TRENDS AND POLICY OPTION

HELPING TO
ELIMINATE POVERTY
THROUGH PRIVATE
INVOLVEMENT IN
INFRASTRUCTURE

Building Bridges

China's Growing Role as Infrastructure Financier for Sub-Saharan Africa

Vivien Foster
William Butterfield
Chuan Chen
Nataliya Pushak

Peru:
Railroad,
Irrigation,
Roads,
Colony Establishment
in AMAZON

THE WORLD BANK

PPIAF

PUBLIC-PRIVATE INFRASTRUCTURE ADVISORY FACILITY

ISBN: 978-0-8213-7554-9
e-ISBN: 978-0-8213-7555-6
DOI: 10.1596/978-0-8213-7554-9

Library of Congress Cataloging-in-Publication Data
Foster, Vivien, 1968-
  Building bridges: China's growing role as infrastructure financier for Africa / Vivien Foster, William Butterfield, and Chuan Chen.
    p. cm. -- (Trends and policy options ; no. 5)
  Includes bibliographical references.
  ISBN 978-0-8213-7554-9 -- ISBN 978-0-8213-7555-6 (electronic)
  1. China--Foreign economic relations--Africa, Sub-Saharan. 2. Africa, Sub-Saharan--Foreign economic relations--China. 3. Investments, Chinese--Africa, Sub-Saharan. 4. Infrastructure (Economics)--Africa, Sub-Saharan. I. Butterfield, William. II. Chen, Chuan. III. Title.
  HF1604.Z4A3574 2008
  338.91'5106--dc22

                                                                2008023785

CONTENTS

BOXES

FIGURES

TABLES

AUTHORS

The authors are, respectively, Vivien Foster, lead economist, Sustainable Development Department, Africa Region of the World Bank; William Butterfield, formerly a consultant to the World Bank; Chuan Chen, lecturer in construction management, University of Melbourne; and Nataliya Pushak, consultant to the World Bank.

ACKNOWLEDGMENTS

This activity was funded by a grant from the Public Private Infrastructure Advisory Facility and undertaken by the Director's Office of the Sustainable Development Department of the Africa Region of the World Bank.

The authors would like to thank all of our World Bank colleagues whose input and advice helped us understand these issues more clearly, including Eleodoro O. Mayorga Alba, Sudeshna Ghosh Banerjee, Philippe Charles Benoit, Harry Broadman, Francisco Galrao Carneiro, Astrid Hillers, Douglass Hostland, Wendy Hughes, Victoria Kwakwa, Charles McPherson, Pierre Pozzo di Borgio, Prasad Tallapragada, Silvana Tordo, Mark Williams, and Whenhe Zhang. We would also like to thank the development agencies that made their procurement data available to us in order to analyze activities of Chinese contractors in projects funded by African Development Bank, Agence Française de Développement, KFW, and the World Bank.

OVERVIEW

In recent years, a number of emerging economies have begun to play a growing role in the finance of infrastructure in sub-Saharan Africa. Their combined resource flows are now comparable in scale to traditional official development assistance (ODA) from Organisation for Economic Co-operation and Development (OECD) countries or to capital from private investors. These non-OECD financiers include China, India, and the Gulf states, with China being by far the largest player.

This new trend reflects a much more positive economic and political environment in sub-Saharan Africa. Real gross domestic product (GDP) growth in the region has been sustained at 4 to 6 percent now for a number of years, and has benefited from an improved investment climate. The rise of the Chinese and Indian economies has fueled global demand for petroleum and other commodities. Africa is richly endowed with these and faces a historic opportunity to harness its natural resources and invest the proceeds to broaden its economic base for supporting economic growth and poverty reduction. In this context, south–south cooperation provides a channel through which the benefits of economic development in Asia and the Middle East can be transferred to the African continent, through a parallel deepening of trade and investment relations.

Chinese finance often goes to large-scale infrastructure projects, with a particular focus on hydropower generation and railways. At least 35 African countries are engaging with China on infrastructure finance deals, with the biggest recipients being Nigeria, Angola, Ethiopia, and Sudan. The finance is channeled primarily through the China Export-Import (Ex-Im) Bank on terms that are marginally concessional, though significantly less so than those associated with ODA. A large share has gone to countries that are not beneficiaries of recent debt relief initiatives. In some cases, infrastructure finance is packaged with natural resource development, making use of a mechanism known as the "Angola mode." Chinese finance is on a scale large enough to make a material contribution toward meeting Africa's vast infrastructure needs. As such, it offers an important development opportunity for the region.

Despite the importance of Chinese finance for African infrastructure, relatively little is known about its value. The main purpose of this study is to quantify the magnitude of these financial flows from China by collating public information from a wide range of Chinese language sources. On this basis, it becomes possible to document the geographic distribution of resources, the types of infrastructure involved, the size and financing terms of the projects, and the modalities through which finance is being provided. The findings raise deeper questions about the economic, social, and environmental impacts of the projects concerned. These lie beyond the scope of this research, but are undoubtedly important and merit future attention.

Value of Chinese Infrastructure Finance

China and Africa have a long history of political and economic ties, which have greatly intensified in recent years. Both bilateral trade and Chinese foreign direct investment (FDI) in Africa grew about fourfold between 2001 and 2005, accompanied by a major influx of Chinese enterprises and workers into the region. The natural resource sector, principally petroleum and to a lesser extent minerals, has been the major focus for both Chinese FDI to Africa and African exports to China. Nevertheless, China remains a relatively small player in Africa's petroleum sector relative to the OECD countries. The growth in commercial activity between China and Africa has been accompanied by a significant expansion of Chinese official economic assistance to the region, which is focused mainly on infrastructure and typically channeled through the China Ex-Im Bank.

To provide a clearer picture of the value and nature of this finance, a database of projects with Chinese finance was constructed, initially based on press reports and subsequently verified from public Chinese language Web sites. The database covers 2001–07. On the basis of this database, it can be estimated that Chinese financial commitments to African infrastructure projects rose from around US$.5 billion per year in 2001–03 to around US$1.5 billion per year in 2004–05, reached at least US$7 billion in 2006—China's official "Year of Africa"—then trailed back to US$4.5 billion in 2007.

About half of the confirmed projects involved Chinese commitments of less than US$50 million. However, Chinese finance has shown itself capable in about half a dozen cases of raising very large contributions of US$1 billion or more in value for single projects. Overall, at least 35 countries in sub-Saharan Africa have benefited from Chinese finance or are actively discussing funding opportunities.

African leadership has typically welcomed China's fresh approach to development assistance, which eschews any interference in domestic affairs, emphasizes partnership and solidarity among developing nations, and offers an alternative development model based on a more central role for the state. However, a number of civil society commentators have expressed concerns about the social and environmental standards applied. The China Ex-Im Bank has its own environmental standards, and its policy is to follow the environmental regulations of the host country.

Sectoral Distribution of Chinese Infrastructure Finance

In terms of sectoral distribution, a large share of the Chinese finance is allocated to general, multisector infrastructure projects, within the framework of broad bilateral cooperation agreements that allow resources to be allocated in accordance with government priorities. However, it is clear that the two largest beneficiary sectors are power (mainly hydropower) and transport (mainly railroads).

In the power sector, China's activities have focused on the construction of large hydropower schemes. By the end of 2007, China was providing at least US$3.3 billion toward the construction of 10 major hydropower projects amounting to more than 6,000 megawatts (MW) of installed capacity. If completed, these schemes would increase the total available hydropower generation capacity in sub-Saharan Africa by around 30 percent. There have also been some activities in thermal generation and transmission, but on a much smaller scale.

China has made a major comeback in the rail sector, with financing commitments on the order of US$4 billion for this sector. They include rehabilitation of more than 1,350 kilometers of existing railway lines and the construction of more than 1,600 kilometers of new railroad. To put this in perspective, the entire African railroad network amounts to around 50,000 kilometers. The largest deals have been in Nigeria, Gabon, and Mauritania.

In the information and communication technology (ICT) sector, China's involvement mainly takes the form of equipment sales to national incumbents, either through normal commercial contracts or through intergovernmental financing tied to purchases of Chinese equipment by state-owned telecom incumbents. An important focus has been the development of national backbone infrastructure. In total in 2001–07, Chinese telecom firms supplied almost US$3 billion worth of ICT equipment, mainly in Ethiopia, Sudan, and Ghana. ~~Task~~

In the road and water sectors, China has been involved in financing a significant number of projects, but the sums involved are much smaller than in the other three sectors; no more than US$900 million overall has gone to the two sectors combined.

Geographic Distribution of Chinese Infrastructure Finance

In terms of geographic distribution, Chinese finance has been highly concentrated, with about 70 percent going to just four countries: Nigeria, Angola, Ethiopia, and Sudan. *oil*

China's involvement in Nigeria, dating back to 2002, began relatively modestly with a number of projects in the telecom and power sectors. A substantial scale-up took place in 2006, when US$5 billion of infrastructure projects were agreed upon, including the 2,600 MW Mambilla hydropower scheme and two major projects to upgrade and modernize the country's railway system. However, the status of these major rail and hydropower projects agreed to in 2006 is currently under review by Nigeria's new administration.

In Angola, Chinese involvement dates back to the peace accords in 2002. The engagement was substantially scaled up in 2004, when a very substantial line of concessional credit was agreed on with the China Ex-Im Bank to allow the government to repair infrastructure and other sectors damaged in the country's 27-year civil war. This US$2 billion loan is known to have been backed by 10,000 barrels per day of oil exports. In 2007, China Ex-Im bank issued another US$2 billion loan to Angola, reportedly devoted entirely to infrastructure needs.

example

China's engagement in Ethiopia amounts to a total of US$1.6 billion. The main focus has been on the ICT sector, particularly the Ethiopia Millennium Project to create a fiber-optic transmission backbone across the country and roll out the expansion of the Global System for Mobile Communication (GSM) network. Most of these were financed under export seller's credit arrangements with the Chinese telecommunications operator ZTE for the supply of equipment to the Ethiopian national telecommunications incumbent.

In Sudan, China has financed close to US$1.3 billion of infrastructure projects, including the development of more than 1,400 MW of thermal generating capacity, the 1,250 MW Merowe hydropower scheme, and a number of other significant investments in the rail and water sectors.

Economic Complementarities

The growing ties between China and Africa, including China's emerging role as a major financier of infrastructure in the region, can be understood in terms of the economic complementarities that exist between the two parties. On the one hand, Africa counts among its development challenges a major infrastructure deficit, with large investment needs and an associated funding gap. China has developed one of the world's largest and most competitive construction industries, with particular expertise in the civil works critical for infrastructure development. On the other hand, as a result of globalization, China's fast-growing manufacturing economy is generating major demands for oil and mineral inputs that are rapidly outstripping the country's domestic resources. Africa is already a major natural resource exporter, and with enhanced infrastructure could develop this potential even further, accelerating economic development in the region.

Meeting Africa's Infrastructure Needs

Sub-Saharan Africa lags behind other developing regions on most standard indicators of infrastructure development, prompting African leaders to call for greater international support in this sphere. By far the largest gaps arise in the power sector, with generation capacity and household access in Africa at around half the levels observed in South Asia and about a third of the levels observed in East Asia and the Pacific. Unreliable power supply leads to losses in industrial production valued at 6 percent of turnover. Furthermore, Africa's limited infrastructure services tend to be much costlier than those available in other regions. For example, road freight costs in Africa are two to four times as high per kilometer as those in the United States, and travel times along key export corridors are two to three times as high as those in Asia. It is estimated that Africa's deficient infrastructure may be costing as much as 1 percentage point per year of per capita GDP growth.

Since 1999, China's construction sector has seen annual growth of 20 percent, making China the largest construction market in the global economy. The competitiveness of Chinese contractors can be gauged by examining how well they fare in international tenders for projects funded by multilateral aid agencies such as the World Bank and the African Development Bank. In recent years, they have accounted for more than 30 percent by value of civil works contracts tendered by these two multilateral agencies, which makes them substantially more successful than contractors of any other nationality. Chinese contractors have been particularly successful in the road and water sectors and in countries such as Ethiopia, Tanzania, and the Democratic Republic of Congo.

Addressing China's Natural Resource Requirements

China's natural resource imports from sub-Saharan Africa reached US$22 billion in 2006. Petroleum alone accounts for almost 80 percent of this trade, with the balance being timber and minerals. As a result, China now depends on Africa for around 30 percent of its oil imports, 80 percent of its cobalt imports and 40 percent of its manganese imports. Overall, Angola is by far the largest trading partner, followed by Republic of Congo, Equatorial Guinea, Sudan, and South Africa.

Even so, it is important to remember that this expansion takes place from a very low base. China's oil companies remain relative latecomers to petroleum exploration and production in Africa. In recent years, China's oil companies have secured oil exploration and drilling rights in Angola, Chad, the Republic of Congo, Côte d'Ivoire, Equatorial Guinea, Ethiopia, Gabon, Kenya, Mali, Mauritania, Niger, Nigeria, São Tomé and Príncipe, and Sudan. However, the US$7.5 billion of Chinese oil sector investments recorded in this study are less than a tenth of the US$168 billion that other international oil companies have already invested in the region. Moreover, most of Africa's oil exports continue to go to OECD countries. Over the 2001–06 period, 40 percent of Africa's oil production was exported to the United States and 17 percent to Europe, compared with 14 percent to China.

Similarly, Chinese companies have secured projects for minerals (including copper, iron, chromium, and bauxite) in countries such as South Africa, Democratic Republic of Congo, Gabon, Guinea, Zambia, and Zimbabwe. The Chinese investment commitments associated with minerals are estimated at around US$3 billion. In some cases, official assistance has simultaneously been used to provide transport and power generation infrastructure needed to facilitate export of minerals such as iron in Gabon or phosphate in Mauritania. However, only 10 percent of Chinese infrastructure finance is directly linked to natural resource exploitation; most of the resources are directed to broader development projects.

Financing Aspects

China's approach to financial assistance is different from that of traditional donors, and forms part of a broader phenomenon of south-south economic cooperation among developing nations. The principles underlying this support are therefore ones of mutual benefit, reciprocity, and complementarities and are grounded in bilateral agreements among states. Unlike traditional ODA, Chinese infrastructure finance is channeled not through a development agency but through the Ex-Im Bank, which has an explicit mission to promote trade. Given the export promotion rationale, the tying of financial support to the participation of contractors from the financing country is a typical feature. A similar approach is being taken by the India Ex-Im Bank and has in the past been used by export credit agencies of other countries.

$/to Africa/goods/not political reasons

The vast majority of infrastructure financing arrangements discussed in this study were financed by the China Ex-Im Bank, which (like any Ex-Im bank) is devoted primarily to providing export seller's and buyer's credits to support the trade of Chinese goods. These credits, along with international guarantees, reached a total of US$26 billion in 2006, making the China Ex-Im Bank one of the largest export credit agencies worldwide. In addition, the China Ex-Im Bank is the only Chinese institution that is empowered to provide concessional loans to overseas projects.

The China Ex-Im Bank is increasingly making use of a deal structure—known as the "Angola mode" or "resources for infrastructure"—whereby repayment of the loan for infrastructure development is made in terms of natural resources (for example, oil). This approach is by no means novel or unique, and follows a long history of natural resource-based transactions in the oil industry. In the case of the China Ex-Im Bank, the arrangement is used for countries that cannot provide adequate financial guarantees to back their loan commitments and allows them to package natural resource exploitation and infrastructure development. The study documents eight resource-backed deals of this kind (including the credit line to Angola) worth more than US$3 billion and covering petroleum, mineral resources, and agricultural products.

The China Ex-Im Bank's terms and conditions are agreed on a bilateral basis, with the degree of concessionality depending on the nature of the project. The World Bank's Debtor Reporting System offers some insight into Chinese lending to sub-Saharan Africa, including both infrastructure and noninfrastructure loans. On average, the Chinese loans offer an interest rate of 3.1 percent, a grace period of 4 years, and a maturity of 13 years. However, there is significant variation around all these parameters across countries with interest rates ranging from 1 to 6 percent, grace periods from 2 to 10 years, and maturities from 5 to 25 years. Measured according to official definitions of concessionality defined by the OECD Export Credit Agreement, and used by the International Monetary Fund (IMF) in The Poverty Reduction and Growth Facility (PRGF) performance criteria and the International Development Association (IDA) in the context of debt sustainability, on average these loans are considered to be nonconcessional including a grant element of only 18 percent relative to a concessionality threshold of 35 percent. Given the wide variation in financial terms across countries, a subset of the loans do fall above the concessionality threshold. In addition to lending, the Chinese Ministry of Commerce's database for Chinese contractors provides some data on grant-funded projects, each of which is typically less than US$30 million in value.

In the context of recent debt relief initiatives, Chinese lending to Africa has prompted a renewed discussion about debt sustainability. A comparison of recent debt relief figures with estimates of potential indebtedness to China suggests that some of the major beneficiaries of Chinese finance, accounting for more than one-third of the total, were countries that did not benefit from Western debt relief initiatives, such as Angola, Sudan, and Zimbabwe. The only beneficiaries of Western debt relief that have contracted relatively large debts to China are Guinea, Mauritania, and Nigeria. It is also worth noting that China has itself provided US$780 million of debt relief to African countries in recent years.

The Wider Landscape

China is by no means the only major emerging financier for infrastructure projects in Africa. India has also been using its Ex-Im Bank to support the development of power projects in countries such as Nigeria and Sudan, where it is developing natural resource interests. Indian infrastructure deals in Africa averaged US$0.5 billion per year in 2003–07, associated with significant natural resource investments. In addition, Arab countries provided an average annual US$0.5 billion for infrastructure finance in Africa in 2001–07. This has taken the form of relatively small projects (on the order of US$20 million) with a heavy emphasis on road investments.

Overall, infrastructure resources provided to Africa by the emerging financiers jumped from around US$1 billion per year in the early 2000s to around US$8 billion in 2006 and US$5 billion in 2007. These flows are now broadly comparable in magnitude to the ODA of OECD donors (amounting to US$5.3 billion in 2006) and to the resources emanating from private participation in infrastructure, or PPI (amounting to more than US$8 billion in 2006).

Resource flows of the magnitude provided by the emerging financiers are large enough to make a material contribution toward meeting Africa's infrastructure financing needs. The contribution is most material in the power sector. In ICT, emerging financiers' contribution is less significant and, moreover, comes on top of already abundant sources of finance from PPI. In transport and water, the contribution of emerging financiers remains relatively small in relation to needs.

Notwithstanding some overlap, there is a significant degree of complementarity in the main areas of focus for each of the three major sources of external finance. PPI seeks the most commercially lucrative opportunities in ICT. Emerging financiers focus on productive infrastructure (primarily power generation and railroads). Traditional ODA focuses on the finance of public goods (such as roads and water supply) and plays a broader role in power system development and electrification. A similar pattern of specialization emerges with respect to geography, with different countries relying to differing degrees on the various sources of finance.

Conclusion

The advent of China and other emerging players as important financiers represents an encouraging trend for Africa, given the magnitude of its infrastructure deficit. The investments made by these emerging financiers are unprecedented in scale and in their focus on large-scale infrastructure projects. With new actors and new modalities, there is a learning process ahead for borrowers and financiers, both new and old alike. Salient issues are the development of national capacity to negotiate complex and innovative deals, and to enforce appropriate environmental and social standards for project development. In sum, the key challenge for African governments is how to make the best strategic use of all external sources of infrastructure funding, including those of emerging financiers, to promote growth and reduce poverty on the continent.

GLOSSARY OF TERMS

Angola mode	A financing scheme in which the repayment of a loan is linked to natural resource exports
Concessional	According to OECD-ECA (Export Credit Agreement) definition, concessional finance is defined as having terms that provide an equivalent grant element of 35 percent or more relative to what can be secured on the commercial market
FDI	Foreign direct investment captures private equity investments of foreign companies
FEC	Foreign economic cooperation captures overseas construction contracts, labor exports, consulting services, and nonfinancial FDI (as such, it does not correspond to either FDI or ODA)
ODA	Official development assistance captures concessional, financing for projects with a clear development purpose
PPI	Private participation in infrastructure captures FDI in infrastructure sectors under contractual arrangements in which the private sector assumes operational responsibilities and bears business risks

ABBREVIATIONS AND ACRONYMS

ASB	Alcatel Shanghai Bell
CAAC	Civil Aviation Administration of China
CABC	China-Africa Business Council
CADF	China Africa Development Fund
CATIC	China National Aero-Technology Import & Export Co.
CCECC	China Civil Engineering Construction Company
CCS	Chambishi Copper Smelter
CCT	China-Congo Telecom
CDB	China Development Bank
CDMA	Code Division Multiple Access
CEIEC	China National Electronics Import and Export Corporation
CGC	China Geo-Engineering Corporation
CGGC	China Gezhouba Group Corporation
CHICO	China Henan International Cooperation Group
CITCC	China International Telecommunication Construction Corporation
CITIC	China International Trust and Investment Corporation
CMEC	China National Machinery & Equipment Import & Export Corporation
CMIC	China Machine-Building International Corporation
CNMC	China Nonferrous Metal Mining (Group) Co. Ltd.
CNOOC	China National Offshore Oil Corporation
CNPC	China National Petroleum Corporation
COVEC	China National Overseas Engineering Corporation
CRBC	China Road and Bridge Corporation
CRCC	China Railway Construction Corporation

CREGC	China Railway Engineering Group Co. Ltd.
CWE	China International Water & Electric Corporation
CWHEC	China National Water Resources and Hydropower Engineering Corporation
DAC	Development Assistance Committee of the OECD
DLX	Dalian Xinyang High-Tech Development
DRC	Democratic Republic of Congo
DRS	Debtor Reporting System
ECCO	Economic and Commercial Counselor's Office
ECA	Export Credit Agreement
Ex-Im Bank	Export-Import Bank
FDI	foreign direct investment
FOCAC	Forum on China-Africa Cooperation
GDP	gross domestic product
GNI	gross national income
GNPOC	Greater Nile Petroleum Operating Company
GPRS	General Packet Radio Services
GSM	Global System for Mobile communications
HPEC	Harbin Power Equipment Company Limited
ICT	information and communication technology
IDA	International Development Association
IFC	International Finance Corporation
IMF	International Monetary Fund
JDZ	Joint Development Zone
JIETDC	Jilin Province International Economy & Trade Development Corporation
JISCO	Jiuquan Iron & Steel Company
JNMC	Jinchuan Group Limited
MOFCOM	Ministry of Commerce of the People's Republic of China
MDG	Millennium Development Goal
MOU	memorandum of understanding
MW	megawatt
NEC	National Electricity Corporation of Sudan
NNPC	Nigerian National Petroleum Corporation
NRPT	National Rural Telephony Project
ODA	official development assistance
OECD	Organisation for Economic Co-operation and Development
ONGC	Oil and Natural Gas Corporation

PPI	private participation in infrastructure
PRGF	The Poverty Reduction and Growth Facility
RII	Rites and Ircon International
SEPCO	Shandong Electric Power Construction Corporation
SINOPEC	China Petroleum and Chemical Corporation
Sino U	China Nuclear International Uranium Corporation
SOE	state-owned enterprise
SONITEL	Niger Telecommunications Company
SSA	Sub-Saharan Africa
SSI	Sonangol Sinopec International
WIETC	Weihai International Economic & Technical Cooperative Co., Ltd
WITS	World Integrated Trade Solution
WSS	Water supply and sanitation
YNCIG	Yunnan Copper Industry (Group) Co. Ltd.
ZPEB	Zhongyuan Petroleum Exploration Bureau
ZTE	Zhong Xing Telecommunication Equipment Company Limited *State-owned*

1.

INTRODUCTION

China and Africa have a long history of political and economic ties, which have greatly intensified in recent years. Both bilateral trade and Chinese foreign direct investment (FDI) in Africa grew about fourfold between 2001 and 2005, accompanied by a major influx of Chinese enterprises and workers into the region. The natural resource sector, principally petroleum and to a lesser extent minerals, has been the major focus for both Chinese FDI to Africa and African exports to China.

This growth in commercial activity between China and Africa has been accompanied by a significant expansion of Chinese official economic assistance to the region, which is focused mainly on infrastructure and typically channeled through the China Export-Import (Ex-Im) Bank. Although this assistance is widely reported in the press, there are no official statistics on its overall value. Various attempts to estimate volumes have been speculative at best, but suggest a multibillion-dollar scale. Given the conclusion of the Commission for Africa that there is a need to double the estimated historical (public and private) financing flows of around US$10 billion per year to Africa's infrastructure development, there is no doubt that the opening of a major new source of infrastructure finance is of material importance for the region.

Chinese official economic assistance often takes the form of loans provided by the China Ex-Im Bank to specific African governments for the development of infrastructure projects. In line with the typical practice of export-import banks, support is partly tied to participation by contractors from the financing country. The resulting infrastructure remains the property of the African governments and their parastatals, which are responsible for the subsequent operation and management of the assets. Reflecting priorities identified by the beneficiary countries, the focus of projects to date has been in the area of productive infrastructure, including power, rail, and information and communication technology (ICT) as well as some high-profile construction projects. While it is known that the China Ex-Im Bank provides a significant volume of concessional financing to Africa for such infrastructure development, the details of the associated financing terms are not typically disclosed.

There is therefore a need for the international community to improve its understanding of the new role that China is playing in the development of Africa's infrastructure, and its implications for Africa's development. The objective of this report is to contribute to such an understanding by providing more solid estimates of the overall volume of finance, as well as an analysis of its composition. The report focuses on sub-Saharan Africa, which is where infrastructure financing needs are particularly critical and where the bulk of the Chinese activity has taken place. The starting point for this endeavor is the construction of a database that documents each of the projects reported to have Chinese financing, which are subsequently verified through a range of Chinese and international sources.

The report is structured along the following lines. Section 2 provides an overview of the growing economic ties between China and Africa, in particular the extent of our current understanding of Chinese infrastructure finance in the region. Section 3 examines the data available from official Chinese government sources and discusses the methodological challenges inherent in quantifying the extent of official assistance for infrastructure finance. Section 4 presents the headline estimates on the value of Chinese finance based on the projects database developed for this report. Section 5 details the economic complementarities that exist between China and Africa, based on Africa's need for infrastructure and China's natural resource import requirements. Sections 6 and 7 present a more detailed profile of Chinese-financed infrastructure projects in Africa on a sector-by-sector and country-by-country basis. Section 8 presents the available information on financing mechanisms and terms, and considers the overall impact on country indebtedness. Section 9 places the phenomenon of Chinese infrastructure finance into a broader international perspective, comparing it with flows provided by traditional OECD financiers and other emerging players such as India and the Arab countries. Finally, section 10 draws out the main conclusions and implications.

2.

CHINA'S GROWING TIES WITH SUB-SAHARAN AFRICA

China's growing economic ties with Africa have attracted increasing interest from the policy community and spawned a burgeoning literature. In just the last year, a wide variety of international agencies and think tanks have published studies documenting different aspects of China's engagement in Africa.[1] The issue has also been discussed by African institutions and civil society organizations (see, for example, the special Pambazuka News Issue in 2006).

The most extensive studies to date have focused on understanding the trade relationships between Asia and Africa, with a particular focus on China (Broadman 2006 and Goldstein et al. 2006). According to IMF Direction of Trade Statistics, by 2007, the total value of trade between China and Africa reached US$59 billion, up from less than US$10 billion in 2001 (figure 1). Africa's exports to China consist mainly of oil, minerals, and other natural resources such as timber, needed to fuel the dramatic growth of China's manufacturing sector. China's exports to Africa consist mainly of manufactured consumer goods. China's share of Africa's trade has jumped from 2 percent to 6 percent, making it the region's third largest trading partner after the United States and France (Alden and Rothman 2006).

---

[1] These include Agence Française de Développement (Jacquet et al. 2007), Carnegie Endowment for International Peace (Kurlantzick 2006), Center for Global Development (Moss and Rose 2006), Center for Strategic and International Studies (Glosny 2006 and Gill et al. 2007), Corporate Council on Africa (Shelton 2005), Department for International Development (University of Stellenbosch 2006), East West Center (Zhang 2006), International Rivers Network (Bosshard 2007), Organisation for Economic Co-operation and Development (Goldstein et al. 2006), and the World Bank (Broadman 2006).

Figure 1: Chinese trade with and foreign direct investment in sub-Saharan Africa

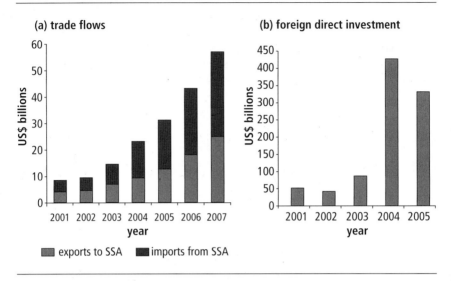

Source: IMF Direction of Trade Statistics (2008) and Ministry of Commerce (2006).

Complementing the growth in trade has been an expansion of Chinese foreign direct investment in Africa, particularly in the natural resource sector. According to the Ministry of Commerce, the volume of Chinese FDI to Africa increased from around US$50 million per year in the early 2000s to around US$400 million per year in 2004–05.

In parallel with the deepening commercial ties described above, a number of authors comment on the substantial growth of official economic assistance provided by China to African governments (see, for example, Glosny 2006 and Kurlantzick 2006), and document the rapid growth of the China Export-Import (Ex-Im) Bank to become one of the world's largest export credit agencies, as well as its emergence as the privileged channel for Chinese overseas concessional lending (Moss and Rose 2006).

Chinese official assistance to Africa has a history dating back to the 1960s. Brautigam (1997) notes that by 1975 China had aid programs in more African countries than did the United States, and that total Chinese aid to Africa over the period 1960 to 1989 has been estimated at US$4.7 billion. During the early decades of the PRC, Chinese aid efforts in Africa focused on small-scale agricultural development projects on highly concessional terms of finance, typically accompanied by transfer of Chinese know-how.

BOX 1

A brief history of Sino-African engagement

China's engagement in Africa goes far back in history and includes trade along the Silk Road (which through the Arab peninsula and India also reached Africa) as well as Admiral Zheng He's travels to eastern Africa in the 15th century.

China's contemporary engagement with Africa has its roots in the mid-1950s, notably in the Bandung Conference, where Asian and African states reinforced nonalignment and sought to promote Afro-Asian economic and cultural cooperation. Chinese Premier Zhou Enlai's tour of 10 African countries between 1963 and 1964 offered support to Africa's people and leaders, and Chinese overseas development assistance became a feature of relations, focusing on infrastructure development as well as technical and student exchange visits (particularly in the field of medicine). The most notable example of the cooperation was construction of the Tazara railway, linking Zambia to the coastal port of Dar es Salaam in Tanzania and thus providing Zambia with an alternative route to the sea.

After Deng Xiaoping's reforms took off in 1978, Sino-African cooperation became less prominent for some time, but regained momentum in the 1990s. President Jiang Zemin, who toured Africa in May 1996, presented the Five Points Proposal establishing the contours of a new relationship with Africa, centering on a reliable friendship, sovereign equality, nonintervention, mutually beneficial development, and international cooperation.

In October 2000, the first Forum on China-Africa Cooperation (FOCAC) was held in Beijing. The forum reached consensus on a wide range of issues and culminated in the adoption of two policy documents—*The Beijing Declaration* and the *Program of Cooperation on Economic and Social Development*. Thereafter, the ministerial conference became a triennial event convened alternately in China and Africa.

(continued)

With the notable exception of the 1,860-kilometer Tanzania-Zambia Railway (Tazara) completed in 1976, Chinese aid during this period did not typically focus on infrastructure. Following the economic reforms of the 1990s, Brautigam notes that there was a major shift in overseas development assistance policy toward a more market-based approach with a move away from zero interest lending, and a greater focus on the economic rationale for aid projects.

This led to a scale-up in financial assistance in the early 2000s with a particular focus on infrastructure projects. Indeed, China's officials declared 2006 China's "Year of Africa," marked by intensive diplomatic outreach, including a series of official visits by the Chinese premier and culminating in the heads of state Forum on China-Africa Cooperation (FOCAC) held in Beijing in October 2006, where the Chinese government pledged US$5 billion dollars of aid to Africa over the next three years. China's African policy highlights "mutual benefit, reciprocity and common prosperity" as a guiding principle for China's activities in the region (King 2006).

Commentators agree that China's role in infrastructure finance in the region is substantial, though no precise figures exist. A few studies have attempted to provide first-order estimates of the value of Chinese finance for African infrastructure projects. At the low end of the spectrum, Agence Française de Développement estimates Chinese financing in the range of US$1.6 billion and US$2.2 billion for 2004 (Chaponniere 2007). They arrive at this conclusion by taking total foreign economic cooperation in Africa of US$2.6 billion for the same year (official Chinese numbers), and netting out both (a) the value of contracts won by Chinese contractors from multilateral agencies and (b) an estimate of private sector activity. At the high end of the spectrum, the Center for Global Development (2006) estimates (based on international press reports) that Chinese-financed infrastructure projects in Africa amounted to at least US$7.5 billion over the period 2004–05. A recent study by Stellenbosch University (2006), while not attempting to provide an overall estimate of the value of Chinese infrastructure finance, does document the existence of a US$2 billion credit line for Angola alone.

Although inconclusive, these estimates point to the substantial scale of Chinese financing. They can be compared, for example, with commitments of around US$5 billion of official assistance to infrastructure projects in sub-Saharan Africa by Organisation for Economic Co-operation and Development (OECD) countries in 2006 (Infrastructure Consortium for Africa, 2007). The Chinese contribution also appears to be material when set against estimates of the overall infrastructure financing needs of sub-Saharan Africa, and the associated funding deficit.

Chinese financing flows typically involve projects implemented by Chinese contractors that are funded through bilateral loans from the China Ex-Im Bank to the government of the beneficiary country. Because the Chinese contractors involved do not risk equity capital nor gain control over any foreign affiliate, the loans do not qualify as FDI. While the financing terms are often described as concessional, exact details are not typically reported. Thus, it is not clear whether or not they would qualify as concessional based on the OECD's official definition of official development assistance (ODA), which entails "flows to developing countries provided by official agencies which have a clear development purpose and are at least partially concessional in nature."

Comparisons with traditional ODA can be misleading. On the one hand, traditional ODA constitutes concessional finance from high-income countries to lower-income countries for development purposes, usually delivered through bilateral or multilateral aid agencies with an explicit mission to reduce poverty in the recipient country. These flows are guided by the agreements made under the OECD Development Assistance Committee, which over a number of decades has sought to reform practice to ensure that ODA delivers the maximum benefit to the recipient country, for example, by untying contracts, developing safeguards, and harmonizing procedures. On the other hand, support from emerging players such as China (and India) constitutes official financing *between* lower-income countries, and is delivered not through development agencies, but rather through Ex-Im banks with an explicit mission to promote trade and development in the originating country. Given the lower income level of the originating country, it makes sense that this financing is designed to bring benefits to the financier as well as to the borrower. The export promotion logic of the financing provided also explains the prevalent practice of tying this to contractors from the financing country, which is standard for Ex-Im banks.

African leadership has typically welcomed China's fresh approach to development assistance, which eschews any interference in domestic affairs and emphasizes partnership and solidarity among developing nations (King 2006; Pambazuka 2006). However, a number of civil society commentators have expressed concerns about the social and environmental standards applied in Chinese-funded projects in Africa (Alden and Rothman 2006; Bosshard 2007, 2008; Glosny 2006; Kurlantzick 2006; Pambazuka 2006). These relate primarily to the import of Chinese laborers and the resettlement procedures associated with the construction of large dams. China Ex-Im Bank has its own environmental standards; its policy is to respect the environmental regulations of the host country. At the same time, the Chinese approach is seen to provide a viable alternative development model based on a much more central role for the state that often appeals to African governments (Gill et al. 2007).

3.

METHODOLOGY

Estimating the extent of Chinese financing of infrastructure project in Africa presents numerous methodological challenges because official Chinese data sources do not produce figures at the level of disaggregation required to document this specific issue.[2]

Existing Information Sources

The China Export-Import (Ex-Im) Bank, which is the main financier of Chinese infrastructure projects in Africa, publishes data on the overall volume of its export financing. The total value of commitments for worldwide export credits and guarantees, pegged at close to US$26 billion in 2006,[3] has quadrupled since the year 2000. However, data on concessional lending—the relevant financing mode for African infrastructure projects—are not typically disclosed.

The Ministry of Commerce publishes annual statistics on "foreign economic cooperation," which is a broad concept encompassing the value of overseas contracts, labor exports, consulting services, and nonfinancial foreign direct investment. These statistics, which are broken down at the country level, indicate that new contractual commitments to projects in sub-Saharan Africa tripled from just under US$2 billion in 2002 to just over

---

[2] Statements about the value of Chinese aid are occasionally made by senior political figures but are difficult to interpret or reconcile with respect to officially determined categories.

[3] Includes approved US$17.5 billion of export seller's credits, US$4.24 billion of export buyer's credits, and US$4.4 billion of international guarantees (from China Ex-Im Bank's annual report 2006, http://english.Ex-Imbank.gov.cn/annual/reportall.jsp, pp. 19–23).

Figure 2: Chinese foreign economic cooperation in sub-Saharan Africa, 2002–05

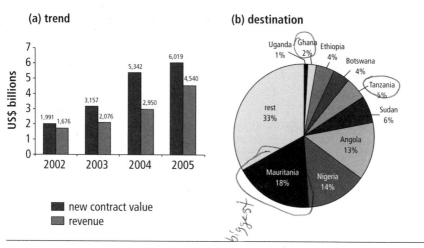

(a) trend

(b) destination

Source: Ministry of Commerce, PRC (2006).

US$6 billion in 2005 (figure 2a). Around half of this cooperation went to four countries: Mauritania, Nigeria, Angola, and Sudan (figure 2b).

These official statistics on foreign economic cooperation merge together three distinct types of projects: those financed from official Chinese sources (which are of central interest to this study), those undertaken by Chinese contractors but financed by multilateral agencies (such as the World Bank), and those undertaken by Chinese enterprises in association with overseas private contractors (AFD 2006). It is possible to make some crude adjustments to these figures to get closer to a true approximation of the likely value of Chinese-financed projects by subtracting from these totals the known value of Chinese FDI in sub-Saharan Africa, as well as the known value of multilateral contracts awarded to Chinese firms, over the same period (table 1). This yields estimates that increase from US$1.8 billion in 2002 to US$5.3 billion in 2005. Data for 2006 were not available at the time of writing. This figure provides a likely upper bound for Chinese government–financed infrastructure projects in the region, because in addition to network infrastructure this will include other construction projects that China has undertaken in Africa, including sports stadiums and residential housing, as well as presidential palaces and parliamentary buildings.

Finally, during a six-nation tour of Africa in June of 2006, Premier Wen Jiabao said China has offered more than US$44 billion in aid over the past 50

Table 1: Estimated upper bound of Chinese infrastructure finance commitments in sub-Saharan Africa, 2002–05 (US$ millions)

	2002	2003	2004	2005
Foreign economic cooperation in sub-Saharan Africa	1,869.2	3,128.6	5,283.9	5,941.0
Less				
Chinese FDI in sub-Saharan Africa	62.8	107.4	432.0	345.6
Value of multilateral contracts in sub-Saharan Africa secured by Chinese contractors	30.2	24.0	259.9	276.2
Yields				
Estimated upper bound of Chinese infrastructure finance commitments in sub-Saharan Africa	1,776.2	2,997.2	4,592.0	5,319.2

Sources: Ministry of Commerce, World Bank, African Development Bank.

years to finance 900 infrastructure projects.[4] In 2005, he stated that the Chinese government provided US$950 million in aid to Africa. During 2007, China's top leaders visited about half of the 48 African countries with which China has diplomatic ties,[5] signing debt relief and aid agreements with 28 countries.[6]

A New Project Database

In view of these difficulties, the approach developed in this paper is to build up a project-by-project estimate of the total value of Chinese infrastructure finance, triangulating from as many different sources as possible and drawing upon both international sources and Chinese sources.

In a first round of data collection, international press reports were systematically reviewed and attempts were made to verify them through World Bank channels.

The starting point was international English language media. The Factiva media database was used to perform a systematic search of newspaper articles

[4] "Benin Offers Incentives to Chinese Companies Exploring for Oil." Dow Jones International News, August 28, 2006.
[5] (2007) AFRICA-CHINA: Hu's Tour Africa Research Bulletin: Economic, Financial, and Technical Series 44 (1), 17243A–17245C doi:10.1111/j.1467-6346.2007.00723.x.
[6] China Ministry of Commerce (http://xyf2.mofcom.gov.cn/aarticle/workaffair/200712/20071205263642.html).

covering Chinese infrastructure projects in Africa over the period 2001–07. Factiva, a Dow Jones & Reuters company, is a database of international newspapers, magazines, and business press releases that uses more than 10,000 different sources. Annex 1 provides a detailed discussion of search terms. The newspaper reports were used to construct project records detailing the date, country, sector, Chinese agency involvement, nature of project, type of financing, amount of financing, and current status. Annex 2 provides a detailed description of the database structure. To understand the linkages between infrastructure projects and natural resource development, a parallel database was created documenting natural resource projects using the same method.

While this approach was effective in generating a rapid overview of projects underway, it suffers from a number of shortcomings. To the extent that the media may cover the initial announcement of a financing commitment, but fail to indicate whether or not the commitment follows through over time, the newspaper reports may be overstating the real extent of Chinese finance. To the extent that the media may focus on larger (more newsworthy) projects, the newspaper reports may be underestimating the extent of Chinese finance by overlooking smaller projects. In some cases, media reports are incomplete, documenting the existence of a project but not providing details on the value of financial commitments.

Subsequently, interviews were undertaken with World Bank operational staff who had direct engagement in the countries and sectors where the projects had been identified through the media search. Through these interviews it was usually possible to establish whether or not the announced projects were actually going ahead, and in some cases the projects' overall value. This provides a first screening of the newspaper material that serves to increase the level of confidence in the reports. In addition, the project list was checked against the World Bank's Debtor Reporting System (DRS) up to 2005, which is based on information provided by borrowing countries on their bilateral debts.

In a second round, Chinese press reports were systematically reviewed and all projects identified from both Chinese and international sources were subjected to a validation process using the official Web sites of the relevant Chinese government institutions and state-owned enterprises.

The Chinese press search was conducted using a powerful Chinese search engine (www.baidu.com), as well as a commercial database, Chinese Journal Web, which consists of different databases such as Chinese Journal Full Article Database (including 7,300 types of Chinese journals from 1994) and Important Chinese Newspaper Full Article Database (including 430 types of Chinese newspapers from 2000). Newspapers proved to be more valuable than journals in providing useful and up-to-date information for this study.

Chinese newspapers can be divided into two categories: national newspapers, including some industry-specific/professional newspapers; and provincial/municipal/private newspapers with a more local or regional focus.

The next stage was to validate press reports by matching them up against information provided through the Web sites of relevant government institutions and state-owned enterprises. In all cases, the information provided from these sources is official in nature and can be regarded as the most reliable and accurate Chinese source of information. However, in some cases, the data are limited in terms of project coverage and level of detail.

First, the Ministry of Commerce of the People's Republic of China (MOFCOM) publishes all foreign aid projects (that is, grant-funded projects) for bidding among Chinese contractors online. The announcement includes the description of the project and the short list of prequalified bidders. The release of the information is required by law.

Second, MOFCOM also has local Economic and Commercial Counselor's Offices (ECCOs) housed within the network of Chinese embassies across Africa. The ECCOs normally have well-maintained Web sites reporting local projects with Chinese involvement, and are in close contact with events on the ground.

Third, the Ministry of Foreign Affairs as well as the State-Owned Assets Supervision and Administration Commission of the State Council also report project-specific information from time to time on their Web sites, especially relating to large projects.

Fourth, as a state policy bank, China Ex-Im Bank reports significant infrastructure projects with concessional loan or export credit-backed projects in its annual report.

The final stage was to look at the Web sites of those Chinese contractors that were identified as being active in Africa through the English language media search. Because only a few of these contractors are listed on stock markets, annual reports are normally unavailable. However, some information can be found from material posted on their corporate Web sites. Although this type of information is the least official among the three, it is considered to be usually reliable.

Nevertheless, in many cases, none of the sources alone provides the whole picture on a specific project, but instead they can be complementary. For example, the contractor may report the cost of a project, but this can be less than what the African government receives from China; hence the importance of conducting cross-checks among the Chinese sources cited.

To summarize, the different methods of data collection and validation described above can be grouped into two categories. The first is the press reports (both Chinese and international), which provide a general picture of what is happening, but which on their own are of questionable accuracy. The second are the official sources, whether World Bank or Chinese government, which are used to cross-check the accuracy of the project details identified through the press.

Figure 3 illustrates the percentage of the full set of investment commitments identified by the Chinese and international press that could be confirmed from different sources. In value terms, it proved possible to verify 76 percent of the financing commitments reported in the press through the various official sources. In numerical terms, however, the percentage of finance commitments cases that could be confirmed is substantially lower, representing only 59 percent of the total number in the original press reports. This finding is not entirely surprising, and simply indicates that it proved harder to verify data on the large tail of small commitments than on the more limited number of large commitments.

Given the uncertainty that exists, the study will take a conservative approach and report *only on projects reported by the Chinese press whose values could subsequently be confirmed from official Chinese sources.* In value terms, 76 percent of the projects identified could be confirmed by Chinese sources, and the remaining 24 percent by international sources only (see figure 3). About 60 percent of the projects' overall value identified could be confirmed both by Chinese and international sources.

However, it is important to note that even the signature of an intergovernmental agreement does not guarantee that the project will eventually go ahead, and there have been some important cases of such projects subsequently being questioned or halted. Moreover, the status of projects under agreement but not yet commenced is often subject to frequent changes so that it is difficult to reach a final verdict on the status of these projects. Unfortunately, it is often some of the larger projects that have the greatest uncertainty associated with them, and this can substantially affect the overall totals. The approach taken here, therefore, is to count all projects that have been confirmed as signed in the totals, but to comment in the text on those projects whose implementation remains in question at the time of writing.

It is important to clarify that all the infrastructure projects captured in the database are projects with official financial assistance and do not constitute FDI. That is to say that the projects are entirely debt financed, typically by the China Ex-Im Bank. There are also some grant projects funded by the Ministry of Commerce. In none of these cases do the enterprises involved put in any of their own equity, which is a key element of the definition of FDI. The only possible area of ambiguity relates to the projects (a) equity financed by

Figure 3: Chinese-financed infrastructure projects in sub-Saharan Africa that could be validated from different sources, 2001–07

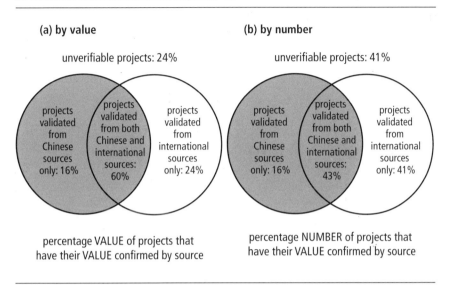

(a) by value

unverifiable projects: 24%

projects validated from Chinese sources only: 16%

projects validated from both Chinese and international sources: 60%

projects validated from international sources only: 24%

percentage VALUE of projects that have their VALUE confirmed by source

(b) by number

unverifiable projects: 41%

projects validated from Chinese sources only: 16%

projects validated from both Chinese and international sources: 43%

projects validated from international sources only: 41%

percentage NUMBER of projects that have their VALUE confirmed by source

Source: World Bank–PPIAF Chinese Projects Database (2008).

the China Africa Development Fund, established by the China Development Bank as a commercial financing institution (Davies et al. 2008) and (b) financed directly by Chinese state-owned companies, without recourse to official financing sources (although oftentimes availability of such a recourse is plausible but cannot be confirmed). However, these account for only about 5 percent of the values under consideration (see figure 15).

In later sections, the paper also presents some estimates of Chinese funding for natural resource development in sub-Saharan Africa. These constitute equity flows by Chinese (private and state-owned) corporations and can therefore properly be considered FDI.

Finally, all the values reported throughout this paper relate to financing commitments rather than actual disbursements. This is common practice in the reporting of official development assistance financing.

4.

THE EMERGENCE OF CHINESE INFRASTRUCTURE FINANCE

Based on the methodology described in the previous section, this section presents estimates of the total envelope of Chinese official financing commitments for infrastructure projects in sub-Saharan Africa. More detail is then provided concerning the sectoral and geographic composition of the projects identified.

Headline Numbers

Applying the methodology described in the previous section, it is possible to provide estimates for the total volume of Chinese finance for infrastructure projects in Africa. It is relevant to note that the estimates presented here are well within the upper bound determined through the official statistics on Foreign Economic Cooperation presented in the previous section (see table 1).

The findings are that new commitments of Chinese infrastructure finance, which had oscillated around US$500 million per year in the early 2000s, grew substantially after 2003, stepping up to around US$1.3–1.7 billion per year in 2004 and 2005, topping US$7 billion in 2006 (which was the Chinese "Year of Africa"), and tailing back to around US$4.5 billion in 2007 (figure 4).

It is interesting to compare these confirmed financing figures with the total envelope reported in the press. This evidently cannot be regarded as an estimate of actual finance, but provides a good barometer of the intensity of deal-making activity. The correspondence between press reports and confirmed estimates is relatively close except for 2006, when a divergence on the order of US$2.3 billion (or 25 percent) opened up between the two (see figure 4). This no doubt reflects the intense coverage of Chinese activities in Africa prompted by high-level intergovernmental meetings as part of the Chinese "Year of Africa."

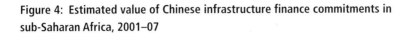

Figure 4: Estimated value of Chinese infrastructure finance commitments in sub-Saharan Africa, 2001–07

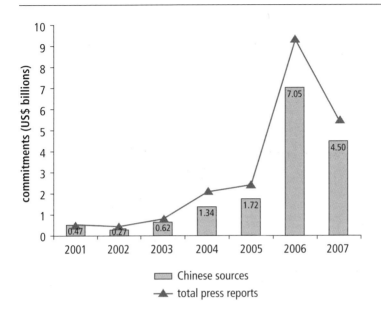

Source: World Bank–PPIAF Chinese Projects Database (2008).

The number of projects has been close to 30 per year in the last few years compared to fewer than 10 per year in the early 2000s (figure 5a). The number of projects reported in the press has tended to be about 50 percent higher on average. This reflects the existence of a large tail of small projects that could not be readily verified through official sources.

The size distribution of the identified infrastructure projects with Chinese finance is skewed toward a large number of relatively small projects of less than US$50 million in value (figure 5b). Nevertheless, there are some half a dozen megaprojects of US$1 billion or more in value, demonstrating the ability of Chinese financing sources to raise very large contributions to individual projects. Overall, at least 35 countries in sub-Saharan Africa have benefited from Chinese finance or are actively discussing funding opportunities.

The financing values reported above relate only to projects on which some formal agreement has been reached or that are further along in the project pipeline. Status is classified according to one of the following mutually exclusive categories: "agreed," "under construction," "completed," or "under

Figure 5: Number and size distribution of Chinese-financed infrastructure projects in sub-Saharan Africa, 2001–07

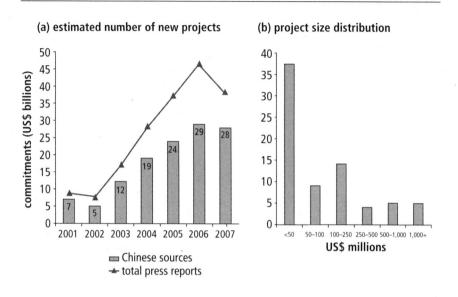

(a) estimated number of new projects

(b) project size distribution

◼ Chinese sources
▲ total press reports

Source: World Bank–PPIAF Chinese Projects Database (2008).

reconsideration." The "agreed" projects are those for which some kind of formal intergovernmental memorandum of understanding (MOU) has been signed. The projects "under construction" are those for which implementation has already commenced, and the "completed" projects are those that have already been finished. Finally, the "under reconsideration" category refers to projects that have been agreed but are for some reason paralyzed in implementation.

Table 2 shows the Chinese finance commitments for all confirmed projects by the year the commitment was made and the status of the project at the end of 2007.

Overall, about 35 percent of the projects by value are either completed or under construction, a further 31 percent have been agreed on but not yet initiated, and the remaining 34 percent are classified as "under reconsideration." The latter category relates primarily to some major power and rail projects in Nigeria that are currently being reassessed by that country's

Table 2: Chinese financing commitments into infrastructure projects in sub-Saharan Africa, by year of commitment and status at end of 2007 (US$ millions)

Status at end of 2007	2001	2002	2003	2004	2005	2006	2007	Cumulative total 2001–07
Agreed	0	0	0	500	780	858	2,787	4,926
Under construction	280	250	400	180	733	487	1,709	4,039
Completed	194	19	224	660	206	200	0	1,503
Under reconsideration	0	0	0	0	0	5,500	0	5,500
Total	474	269	624	1,340	1,720	7,045	4,496	15,968

Source: World Bank–PPIAF Chinese Projects Database (2008).

authorities and to Souapiti Dam in Guinea. The projects documented in this report have been largely implemented by Chinese contractors. Table 3 identifies the 10 largest Chinese project contractors for the official finance projects included in this study, detailing the estimated volume and distribution of their activity. In the power sector, there are numerous significant players, including Sinohydro, Gezhouba Group, Shandong, and CATIC. In the transport sector, CCECC, China Guangdong Xinguang, and Transtech are the three largest players. In the information and communication technology (ICT) sector, the key player is the state-owned ZTE.

Sector-by-Sector View

Regarding the sectoral distribution of confirmed financing commitments, the share of about 14 percent went to "general" infrastructure projects without any clearly identified sectoral allocation, including the US$2 billion line of credit earmarked for multiple infrastructure projects in 2007. Of the remaining financing commitments, about 33 percent went to electricity, 33 percent to transport, and 17 percent to telecom. Therefore, it appears safe to say that most of China's activities were divided fairly evenly between two main sectors: power (especially hydropower) and transport (especially railroads), followed by the ICT sector (mainly equipment supply). Water projects attracted the least amount of activity.

A more extensive profile of Chinese-funded projects in each of the major infrastructure sectors is provided below. In addition, the sectoral tables in annex 3 provide details of the individual projects recorded in each sector.

Table 3: Top 10 Chinese infrastructure project contractors active in sub-Saharan Africa, 2001–07

	Total value (US$ m)	Sectors	Major countries
China Civil Engineering Construction Corporation (CCECC)	2,500	Transport	Nigeria
China Hydraulic and Hydroelectric Construction Group Corporation (Sinohydro Corporation)	2,242	Electricity	Congo, Dem. Rep. of; Congo, Rep. of; Ghana; Guinea; Sudan; Togo
Zhong Xing Telecommunication Equipment Company Limited (ZTE)	2,101	Telecom	Angola; Central African Republic; DRC; Côte d'Ivoire; Ethiopia; Ghana; Kenya; Lesotho; Mali; Mauritania; Niger; Nigeria; Sudan
China Geo-Engineering Corporation (CGC)	1,024	Electricity, water	Cameroon; Nigeria
China Guangdong Xinguang International Group	1,000	Transport	Nigeria
China Gezhouba Group Corporation (CGGC)	1,000	Electricity	Nigeria
Shandong Electric Power Construction Corporation (SEPCO)	810	Electricity	Sudan, Nigeria
China National Machinery & Equipment Import & Export Corporation (CMEC)	721	Electricity, transport, telecom	Angola; Congo, Rep. of; Ethiopia; Nigeria; Sudan; Senegal; Zimbabwe
Transtech Engineering Corporation	620	Transport	Mauritania
China National Aero-Technology Import & Export Co. (CATIC)	500	Electricity	Zimbabwe

Source: World Bank–PPIAF China Projects Database (2008).

Note: Total value is the sum of the project total Chinese financing commitments for all the projects the contractor is involved with.

Power

The sector attracting the largest amount of Chinese financing has been the power sector, with more than US$5.3 billion in cumulative commitments at present.

Much of this effort has been concentrated in hydroelectric schemes. As of the end of 2007, the Chinese were involved in financing 10 major dams in 9 different African countries. The total cost of these projects is estimated to be more than US$5 billion, of which the Chinese were financing over US$3.3 billion. The combined generating capacity of these plants amounts to more than 6,000 megawatts (MW) of electricity, a significant fraction of the 17,000 MW of hydropower generating capacity that exists today in Africa. Indeed, four of these projects will more than double the total electricity-generating capacity in the host countries where they are located.

The largest hydropower project on this list is the 2,600 MW Mambilla scheme in Nigeria, implementation of which is now uncertain. The second largest is the 1,250 MW Merowe Dam in Sudan, already at an advanced stage of construction. In Zambia, too, more than 1,000 MW of hydropower capacity is being developed between the Kafue Lower Gorge and Kariba North projects.

In 2006, the China Export-Import (Ex-Im) Bank expressed an interest in financing Mphanda Nkuwa dam on the Zambezi River in Mozambique. In September 2007, the six-year 1,200 MW project with an estimated cost of US$2.3–3.2 billion was awarded to the Brazilian operator Camargo Correa and partners who have yet to choose the project's financiers.

Natural resources are being used to secure some of the financing. The Congo River Dam in the Republic of Congo and Bui Dam in Ghana, which are currently under construction, are being financed by the China Ex-Im Bank loans backed by guarantees of crude oil in case of the Congo River Dam, and cocoa, in the case of Bui Dam. The Poubara hydropower dam in Gabon is to be built by Sinohydro as part of the US$3 billion Belinga Iron Ore project; however, the amount of Chinese financing committed into the project is not known. Finally, the loan for the Souapiti Dam in Guinea will supposedly be linked to mining (bauxite) revenues. Despite the fact that an MOU for the construction of the dam was signed in 2006 by Guinea authorities, China Ex-Im bank, and Sinohydro, the current status of the deal remains unclear.

Outside of hydropower, China has also been active in building thermal power stations, the most significant of which have been in Sudan and Nigeria. In 2005, the Shandong Electric Power Construction Corporation agreed to build three separate thermal power stations in Sudan: a 500 MW coal-fired

Figure 6: Confirmed Chinese infrastructure finance commitments in sub-Saharan Africa by sector, 2001–07

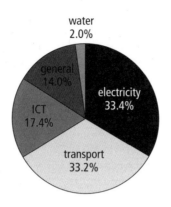

Source: World Bank–PPIAF Chinese Projects Database (2008).

power plant in Port Sudan, a 300 MW gas-fired power plant in Al-Fulah, and a 320 MW gas-fired power plant in Rabak. Earlier, the Harbin Power Equipment Company had agreed to build the E1-Gaili Combined Cycle Power Plant. In Nigeria, the federal government is constructing, with the help of a credit line from China Ex-Im Bank, three gas-fired power stations: Papalanto (335 MW) in Ogun state developed by Shandong Electric Construction Corporation (SEPCO); Omotosho (335 MW) in Ondo, developed by China National Machinery & Equipment Import & Export Corp. (CMEC); and Geregu (138 MW) in Kogi state developed by Siemens.

Other than electricity generation, Chinese companies CMEC and China Machine-Building International Corporation (CMIC) have occasionally gotten involved in electricity transmission through major projects in Tanzania and Luanda (Angola), respectively.

Thus, at present, China's central focus is on the construction of large hydropower projects. Given the current power supply crisis in Africa, and the fact that the region has developed barely 5 percent of its identified hydro potential, these schemes are critical for Africa's economic development. In that sense, the emergence of China as a major financier of hydro schemes is a trend of great strategic importance for the African power sector.

Rail

As stated earlier (see box 1), China began its foray into Africa in large part through the construction of the Tanzania-Zambia railway in the 1970s. In 2001, China pledged continued financial support for the railway; however, it was not possible to confirm whether this led to any definitive agreements.

In recent years, China has made a major comeback in the African rail sector, with financing commitments on the order of US$4 billion for this sector. They include rehabilitation of more than 1,350 kilometers of existing railway lines and the construction of more than 1,600 kilometers of new railroad. To put this in perspective, the entire African railroad network amounts to around 50,000 kilometers. The largest deals have been in Nigeria, Gabon, and Mauritania.

In Nigeria, the Chinese have committed to financing construction of the Abuja Rail Mass Transit System, and to rehabilitation of 1,315 kilometers of the Lagos-Kano line under the first phase of Nigeria railway modernization program. The total cost of the Lagos-Kano rail project is estimated to be US$8.3 billion, of which the Chinese were to cover US$2.5 billion through a line of credit part of which would be also be allocated to support power projects. However, these rail projects agreed under an earlier administration are under review by the Nigerian authorities and their final status is therefore unclear.

China Ex-Im Bank is also preparing to finance the 560 km Belinga-Santa Clara railway in Gabon, which, together with Poubara hydropower dam and deepwater port at Santa Clara, is part of the already mentioned Belinga Iron Ore project. The China Ex-Im Bank's loan for the project is to be repaid via sales of iron ore to China.

The most recent railway project was the commitment to finance a 430 km railroad linking Nouakchott to phosphate-rich Bofal in Mauritania, which was agreed upon in 2007. The project is financed by a US$620 million China Ex-Im Bank loan and will be implemented by Chinese Transtech Engineering Corporation.

Roads

The Chinese have been active in building roads across Africa. The database has recorded more than 18 projects involving Chinese commitments for construction and rehabilitation of more than 1,400 kilometers of road. However, the aggregate value of finance for confirmed projects at around US$550 million is substantially below that reported for the other sectors. The road projects that Chinese firms have undertaken have been relatively small compared to average project sizes in other sectors, and many of them are financed by grants from the Ministry of Commerce. Indeed, the database recorded only two road projects financed by Chinese sources that were larger than US$100 million in size, both of which were in Angola and part of the Ex-Im Bank line of credit provided in 2004. Road building has been an especially important activity in Ethiopia and Botswana. By far the most active Chinese road construction firm was the China Road and Bridge Corporation (CRBC).

Information and Communication Technology

The ICT sector attracted a cumulative total of almost US$3 billion of finance in 2001–07. China's involvement in the ICT sector in Africa mainly takes the form of equipment sales. In some cases, this involves normal commercial contacts between Chinese manufacturers and public and private operators in Africa. However, in some cases, it entails intergovernmental financing tied to purchases of Chinese equipment by state-owned telecom incumbents. While international attention has tended to focus on Africa's new private operators such as Vodacom, MTN, and Celtel, Chinese firms are emerging as key players in the supply of technology and equipment for networks, typically to national telecom incumbents.

By far the largest ICT project has been in Ethiopia (US$1.5 billion), which involved the rollout of national communication backbones and associated rollout of mobile coverage in rural areas. The four-year project, which was initially agreed upon in 2006, was to be undertaken by ZTE, Huawei, and China International Telecommunication Construction Corporation (CITCC). It is expected that, if completed, the project will more than double the country's optical fiber deployment, more than triple mobile network expansion capacity, double rural telecom coverage, and quadruple the length of the fixed telephone network. In 2007, ZTE commenced construction of the first two phases of the project.

The three most active Chinese telecom equipment supply firms were state-owned ZTE, privately held Huawei, and the mixed, private-public, 50-50 French-Chinese joint venture Alcatel Shanghai Bell. In most of the cases recorded by the database, the state-owned Chinese banks directly provided the funds for the equipment to the host government. In some cases, ZTE was able to finance its deals through a standing line of credit with China Ex-Im Bank of US$500 million, issued in 2004. Similarly, Huawei was granted US$600 million export seller's credit from China Ex-Im bank, as well as US$10 billion in credit financing from the China Development Bank, both in 2004. It is important to stress that these lines of credit were given to the contractor firms for their worldwide operations.

A salient example of China's ICT projects is the National Communication Backbone Infrastructural Project in Ghana, agreed to in June of 2006, whereby the China Ex-Im Bank is financing US$31 million of a US$70 million project initiated by the Ministry of Communications through a concessional loan. The project is aimed at rehabilitating and expanding fixed-line communications technology in the country.

Water and Sanitation

Water and sanitation account for a relatively small share of China's total financial commitments to African infrastructure development. Participation in confirmed projects was about US$120 million, and another estimated US$200 million went into Angola's water sector as part of the China Ex-Im Bank credit line of 2004. Most of these projects were smaller scale in nature and more focused on meeting immediate social needs. China's water supply projects include a number of smaller dams that are not related to hydropower but directly to water supply, in Cape Verde and Mozambique.

Country-by-Country View

The projects database records cases of Chinese infrastructure finance for which the amount of commitments was available and confirmed in 27 countries across sub-Saharan Africa. Nevertheless, despite this broad reach in practice, there is a heavy geographic concentration of finance. Four countries—Nigeria, Angola, Ethiopia, and Sudan—together account for about 70 percent of Chinese financing commitments, and Nigeria alone for nearly 30 percent (figure 7). Three other countries—Guinea, Ghana, and Mauritania—have received sizable volumes, on the order of US$0.8–1.0 billion each.

A more extensive profile of the Chinese portfolio of infrastructure projects in each of the four largest recipient countries is provided below. In addition, the country tables in annex 4 provide details of the individual projects recorded in each country.

Nigeria

China's engagement in Nigeria amounts to total financing commitments of US$5.4 billion. The initiation of activities dates back to 2002 with the agreement on the first phase of the National Rural Telephony Project (NRPT), when China's two telecom giants ZTE and Huawei began actively pursuing equipment supply and network rollout projects for both fixed and wireless services in the country.

Nigeria's first loan from the China Ex-Im Bank came in 2005 to support construction of power stations at Papalanto (335 MW), Omotosho (335 MW), and Geregu (138 MW) in Ogun, Ondo, and Kogi states. The construction of Papalanto plant, financing commitments to which we were able to confirm via Chinese sources, was undertaken by Shandong Electric Power Construction Corporation (SEPCO) of China while the China Ex-Im Bank

Figure 7: Confirmed Chinese infrastructure finance commitments in sub-Saharan Africa by country, 2001–07

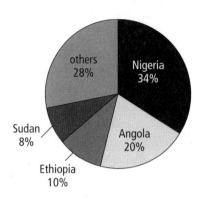

Source: World Bank–PPIAF Chinese Projects Database (2008).

agreed to finance US$300 million of the estimated US$400 million construction costs. The deal was oil-backed such that in return CNPC (or PetroChina, which is CNPC's listed arm) secured a deal to purchase 30,000 barrels of crude oil a day from the Nigerian National Petroleum Corporation (NNPC) for one year, renewable.

In 2006, there was a substantial scale-up in China Ex-Im Bank financing, with almost US$5 billion of projects agreed on. These included contributions of US$2.5 billion to a major Lagos-Kano railway upgrading project; contribution of US$1 billion to Abuja Rail Mass Transit project, which involves the construction of a high-speed rail link between Lagos and Abuja, as well as a light railway system connecting Murtala Mohammed International Airport and Nmandi Azikwe International Airport with the Lagos and Abuja city centers respectively; and a contribution of US$1 billion to the 2,600 MW Mambilla Hydropower project. Following the change of administration in Nigeria, the major rail and power projects are under review by the authorities, and it is not yet clear whether they will go forward.

Angola

China's involvement in infrastructure finance in Angola began in 2002—following the conclusion of the civil war—with a series of relatively small projects involving the rehabilitation of power transmission infrastructure and the installation of a new fiber-optic link.

In 2004, China substantially scaled up its involvement in Angola with the agreement of a China Ex-Im Bank line of credit to allow the government to repair infrastructure damaged in the country's 27-year civil war that formally ended in 2002. The overall size of the line of credit was US$2 billion; however, only half of it went toward infrastructure (electricity, roads, water, telecom, and public works), with the other half dedicated to health, education, and fisheries. This line of credit was disbursed in two equal installments over the 2004–06 period.

The mentioned 2004 US$2 billion loan was backed by an agreement to supply China with 10,000 barrels of Angolan crude per day. Indeed, this type of natural resource-backed financing deal (of which this was the first major example) has come to be known as "Angola mode." The Centre for Chinese Studies at Stellenbosch University indicates that the interest on the loan has been lowered to 0.25 percent from an initial level of more than 1 percent, and that the loan has a 3-year grace period and 15-year repayment term (Corkin, 2006).

Tied to the Chinese loan was the agreement that the public tenders for the construction and civil engineering contracts would be awarded primarily (70 percent) to Chinese state-owned enterprises approved by the Chinese government. In response, the China Ex-Im Bank compiled a list of 35 Chinese companies approved by both the bank and the Chinese authorities to tender in Angola.

In 2007, China Ex-Im Bank issued another US$2 billion loan reportedly devoted entirely to infrastructure needs.

Ethiopia

China's engagement in Ethiopia amounts to US$1.6 billion. Activities began in 2002 with an agreement for construction of the 300 MW Tekeze Dam in the state of Tigray with a total cost of US$224 million, of which China Ex-Im Bank committed US$50 million. Construction is expected to be completed in 2008.

In 2003, Ethiopia saw a number of relatively small-scale projects concentrated in the roads sector, with particular emphasis on improving the city ring road for Addis Ababa. There have also been a couple of significant recent projects for extension of power transmission lines.

However, the main thrust of Chinese financing in the country has focused on the ICT sector, which has absorbed more than 95 percent of the total envelope. Financing was agreed to in 2006–07 for the US$1.5 billion Ethiopia Millennium Project to create a fiber-optic transmission backbone across the country and roll out the expansion of the Global System for Mobile communications (GSM) network, with estimated 8,500,000 new connections. Unlike the earlier projects, most of which have been financed through loans, these were financed under export sellers' credit arrangements with the Chinese telecommunications operator ZTE for the supply of equipment to the Ethiopian national telecommunications incumbent.

Sudan

Since 2001, China has provided US$1.3 billion to the finance of infrastructure projects in Sudan. The early infrastructure projects were all related to the power sector, beginning with construction of the El Gaili Combined Cycle Power Plant in 2001 (followed by expansion in 2007), and the Qarre I thermal station in 2002 (financing for which however was not confirmed by Chinese sources). China later agreed to finance three substantial thermal generation projects for coal-fired and gas-fired stations in Port Sudan, Al-Fulah, and Rabak. Thus, a total of more than 1,400 MW of new thermal generating capacity are being added with Chinese support.

By far the highest-profile power sector project is the ongoing construction of the 1,250 MW Merowe Dam that began in early 2004. This massive US$1.2 billion hydropower project was the largest international project that China had ever participated in at the time the contracts were signed (although it has now been superseded by the Mambilla hydropower project in Nigeria, which will be more than twice the size). Financers of the project included the China Ex-Im Bank (US$400 million), the Saudi Fund (US$150 million), BADEA (US$100 million), the Kuwait Fund for Arab Economic Development (US$100 million), and the Abu Dhabi Fund (US$100 million). The Chinese company Sinohydro was involved in the construction of the plant, while, Harbin Power Equipment Company Limited and Jilin Province Transmission and Substation Project Company took over construction of the 1,776 kilometers of transmission lines within the same project. The government in Khartoum announced that part of the benefits of this dam would be a major increase in the country's electrification rate following much needed investments in distribution. The project has entailed the resettlement of 55,000 to 70,000 residents away from the fertile agricultural areas surrounding the River Nile.

5.

ECONOMIC COMPLEMENTARITIES BETWEEN CHINA AND SUB-SAHARAN AFRICA

The growing economic ties between China and Africa, including China's emerging role as a major financier of infrastructure in the region, can be understood in terms of the evident economic complementarities that exist between the two parties (table 4). On the one hand, Africa counts among its development challenges a major infrastructure deficit, with large investment needs and an associated financing gap. China has developed one of the world's largest and most competitive construction industries, with particular expertise in the civil works critical for infrastructure development. On the

Table 4: Economic complementarities between China and sub-Saharan Africa

	Infrastructure	Resources
Africa	Africa has a major infrastructure deficit.	Africa is a major exporter of natural resources, with infrastructure bottlenecks preventing full realization of its potential
China	China has a large, globally competitive construction industry.	China's manufacturing-based economy creates high demand for natural resource inputs, beyond those domestically available.

Source: Authors.

Table 5: Indicators of infrastructure development in sub-Saharan Africa and other developing regions

Indicator	Sub-Saharan Africa	South Asia	East Asia and Pacific	Europe and Central Asia	Latin America and Caribbean	Middle East and North Africa
Transport						
Paved road density	49	149	59	335	418	482
Total road density	152	306	237	576	740	599
ICT						
Mainline teledensity	33	39	90	261	197	100
Mobile teledensity	101	86	208	489	350	224
Internet density	3	2	7	16	14	10
Power						
Generation capacity	70	154	231	970	464	496
Electricity access	18%	44%	57%	—	79%	88%
Water and sanitation						
Improved water	63%	72	75	87	90	85
Improved sanitation	35%	48	60	78	77	77

Source: Yepes et al. (2007).

Note: Data correspond to the most recent year available for the quinquennium 2000–05. Road densities measured in kilometers per thousand square kilometers; teledensities measured in subscribers per thousand population; generation capacity measured in megawatts per million population; access to electricity and to improved water and sanitation measured in percentage of households.

— = not available.

other hand, China's fast-growing manufacturing economy is generating major demands for oil and mineral inputs that have rapidly outstripped the country's own domestic resources. Even before China's entry into the market, Africa was a major natural resource exporter, with substantial unrealized potential that is attributable (at least in part) to infrastructure bottlenecks that constrain the development of those resources.

The Infrastructure Side

Sub-Saharan Africa currently lags behind other developing regions on most standard indicators of infrastructure development (table 5). This finding holds across a wide range of indicators including road density, paved road density, electricity generation capacity per capita, and household access to electricity, water, and sanitation. By far the largest gaps arise in the power sector, with generation capacity and household access in Africa at around half the levels observed in South Asia, and about a third of the levels observed in East Asia and Pacific. The story is somewhat different for the information and communication technology (ICT) sector, where Africa significantly outperforms South Asia in both mobile and Internet density and comes relatively close in terms of fixed-line density, although the deficit relative to other regions remains large.

Furthermore, Africa's limited infrastructure services tend to be much more costly than those available in other regions. Road freight tariffs in Africa are two to four times as high per kilometer as those in the United States, and travel times along key export corridors are two to three times as high as those found in Asia. The average effective cost of electricity to manufacturing enterprises in Africa is close to US$0.20 per kilowatt-hour, or around four times as high as industrial rates elsewhere in the world. This reflects both high-cost utility power (costing around US$0.10 per kilowatt-hour), and heavy reliance on emergency back-up generation during frequent power outages (costing around US$0.40 per kilowatt-hour). Telecommunications costs have been falling substantially in recent years, but are still high relative to other developing regions. Mobile and Internet telephone charges in Africa are about four times as high as those found in South Asia, and international call prices are more than twice as high.

Inadequate infrastructure stocks are contributing to Africa's poor performance in terms of economic growth. A recent study by Esfahani and Ramirez (2003) estimates that if Africa had shared East Asia's growth rate in terms of telephones per capita (10 percent versus 5 percent) and electricity generation (6 percent versus 2 percent), its economic growth rate would have been 0.9 percent higher than it was. These results are confirmed although with a very different methodology by Calderon and Serven (2004) for a large sample that includes 20 African countries. Using the methodology developed by Calderon and Serven, Estache (2005) finds that, on average, if Africa had enjoyed Korea's quantity and quality of infrastructure, it would have grown by 1.04 percent per capita more. Many similar estimates are available in the literature, all of which confirm the strong growth payoff from investing in infrastructure.

Deficient infrastructure inflates indirect production costs reducing the competitiveness of exports. In spite of low labor costs, sub-Saharan firms have very low participation in export markets. One of the reasons for this lies in high indirect costs. In the case of strong export performers, indirect costs tend to absorb no more than 10–12 percent of total production costs. By contrast, in sub-Saharan Africa, indirect costs can be as high as 20–30 percent of total production costs. Analysis shows that more than half of these indirect costs are infrastructure related, with 31 percent relating to transport and 19 percent relating to power alone.

need power back up + better transport

need to invest
for others to invest

need to spend #
to make #, not shrink state spending

Surveys indicate that deficient infrastructure is one of the key obstacles to doing business, and a key impediment to foreign direct investment (FDI). Emerging evidence from Enterprise Surveys indicates that a high percentage of businesses in sub-Saharan Africa identify deficient infrastructure as one of the major obstacles to the operation and growth of their enterprises. The specific figures are 48 percent for electricity, and 24 percent for transportation; this can be compared with 30 percent that considered corruption to be a major obstacle to doing business. In Nigeria, for example, as many as 76 percent of firms listed electricity as one of the top three constraints to their operations. Recent studies also show that countries with larger infrastructure stocks tend to be more successful at attracting FDI.

A particular problem is the unreliability of power supply, which has major economic consequences for firms. Reliability of infrastructure services in sub-

Table 6: Impact of unreliable infrastructure services on the productive sector

	Sub-Saharan Africa	South Asia	East Asia and Pacific	Europe and Central Asia	Latin America and Caribbean	Middle East and North Africa
Electricity						
Delay in obtaining electricity connection (days)	34.8	49.0	21.5	20.1	34.2	55.4
Average duration of power outages (hours)	6.8	2.4	5.8	6.2	8.0	3.9
Value lost due to power outages (% of sales)	5.9	7.4	2.8	3.0	4.1	4.4
Firms owning or sharing a generator (% of total)	38.5	52.6	22.0	20.5	19.9	38.7
Telecom						
Delay in obtaining a mainline telephone connection (days)	45.6	50.1	18.4	15.2	35.6	28.0
Water						
Delay in obtaining a water connections (days)	40.4	28.8	21.9	21.1	34.6	56.2
Average duration of insufficient water supply (hours)	14.8	5.0	12.7	8.7	13.4	13.4

Source: The World Bank Group Enterprise Surveys from the period 2002/07 (http://www.enterprise surveys.org)

Note: Data for sub-Saharan Africa are based on evidence from 31 countries and those for other developing regions from 69 countries.

usually during peak of mid-day? no clamori

instead of
state doing so by
Solar + wind
big less cost +
over-
decentralized
raw

Saharan Africa is comparatively worse than elsewhere in the developing world, particularly in the case of power and water supply. Firms in sub-Saharan Africa face significant delays in obtaining connections to electricity, water, or telephony services, and suffer electricity outages for as long as 7 hours and insufficient water supply for 15 hours on average. Power cuts lead to economic losses on the order of 6 percent of sales, prompting around 39 percent of all firms to invest in their own high-cost independent generating facilities (table 6). As a result, the typical weighted average cost of power faced by manufacturing firms (considering both own generation and grid purchases) amounts to around US$0.17 per kilowatt-hour.

Closing Africa's infrastructure deficit will require substantial levels of sustained finance for infrastructure in the region. Infrastructure investment needs for sub-Saharan Africa have been estimated as at least 5 percent of the region's GDP, plus a further 4 percent of regional GDP to cover operation and maintenance. In absolute terms, this amounts to US$22 billion per year of investment needs, and a further US$17 billion for maintenance (table 7). The largest investment needs are in the transport sector (US$9.5 billion or 43 percent of the total), followed by electricity (US$5.2 billion or 23 percent of the total), and water and sanitation (US$4.3 billion or 20 percent of the total). These estimates of investment needs are based on research by World Bank staff, which also provided the underlying basis for similar estimates presented in the 2005 *Report of the Commission for Africa*.

The corresponding absolute annual investment requirement of US$22 billion implies a virtual doubling of current investment levels. In addition, a further US$17 billion would be needed for operation and maintenance of infrastructure, amounting to an overall expenditure requirement of US$40 billion per year.[7] Comparing estimated needs of US$22 billion with estimated historical levels in infrastructure of around US$10–12 billion suggests a financing gap of at least US$10 billion.

Whereas Africa shows a particularly strong unmet demand for infrastructure and for infrastructure finance, China has accumulated very substantial financial reserves and has become a leading global supplier of construction services, with particular expertise in the civil works critical for infrastructure development (Chen et al. 2007). Since 1999, China's construction sector has seen annual growth of 20 percent, making China the largest construction market in the global economy (Stellenbosch University 2006). By the end of 2004, the value of China's overseas engineering projects totaled US$156.3 billion, with a sizable share of this value stemming from infrastructure projects. This has been the outcome of China's "Going Global"

[7] Estache (2005).

Table 7: Estimated annual infrastructure investment and maintenance needs to meet Millennium Development Goals in sub-Saharan Africa, 2005–15 (US$ millions)

	Electricity	Telecom	Transport	WSS	Total
Investment	5,200	3,000	9,500	4,300	22,000
Operation and maintenance	3,100	2,200	8,300	3,500	17,000
Total	8,200	5,200	17,800	7,800	39,000

Source: Estache (2005).

Note: WSS = Water supply and sanitation.

[handwritten annotations: "private monopoly", "public monopoly", "Private public", "Public", "the ✓ ignored category"]

strategy initiated in the 1990s with the aim of increasing the international experience of Chinese firms.

One way of gauging the international competitiveness of the Chinese construction industry is to look at the performance of Chinese firms under open tenders. Multilateral agencies, such as the African Development Bank and the World Bank, require unrestricted international competitive bidding to take place on all significant contracts that they finance. The procurement data from these agencies is publicly available and can be used to calculate the share of contract value going to Chinese firms bidding for projects in different segments of the market. This in turn provides an objective indication of the competitiveness of Chinese construction firms.

In the case of the World Bank, it was possible to establish that since 1999 Chinese contractors have been winning a significant share (10–20 percent) of African infrastructure contracts awarded by the International Development Association. The accumulated contract value won by Chinese contractors was US$738 million over the period 2001–06. While substantial, this figure is much lower than the value of Chinese commitments to infrastructure finance over the same period, which are estimated at more than US$12 billion.

Looking at more recent data from both the World Bank and the African Development Bank, it is evident that the success of Chinese firms has been largely confined to the area of civil works. The presence of Chinese firms is almost nonexistent in the area of consulting services, and minimal in the area of equipment supply where they capture a mere 3 percent of the market. However, in the area of civil works Chinese firms accounted for 31 percent of total contract value over the period of 2005–06.[8]

---

[8] The limited procurement data available from bilateral agencies suggest that the share of contracts going to Chinese firms is substantially lower than for multilaterals. In the case of Germany's KfW, for example, Chinese contractors account for only 5 percent of civil works contract values for infrastructure in sub-Saharan Africa over the last five years. Similarly, France's AFD reports less than US$10 million of Chinese contracts over the last three years.

Figure 8: Percentage value of multilateral civil works contracts in sub-Saharan Africa captured by foreign contractors according to their country of origin, 2005–06

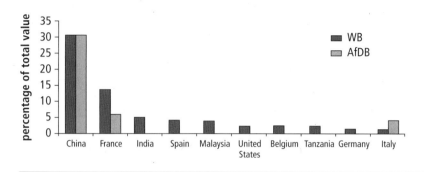

Source: African Development Bank and World Bank procurement data (2005–06).

With the exception of France, which has been winning around 12 percent of World Bank civil works contracts, no other country has won more than a 5 percent share (figure 8). This figure illustrates the competitiveness of Chinese contractors in this market. The World Bank procurement data also provide (partial) information on the nationality of the second most highly ranked bidder for each contract. This shows that in as many as 20 percent of the number of contracts won by Chinese firms, the second most highly ranked bidder is also a Chinese firm.

Chinese firms have tended to capture the larger civil works contracts. The average size of a civil works contract awarded to a Chinese contractor was US$6 million in the case of the African Development Fund window of the African Development Bank and US$11 million in the case of the International Development Association arm of the World Bank, compared to more typical contract values of US$3–4 million.

Within the civil works field, Chinese contractors have been particularly successful winning contracts in the transport (mainly roads) and water sectors—where they captured respectively 38 percent and 32 percent of tenders awarded—compared to only 7 percent in power and none at all in ICT. In terms of sectoral distribution of the civil works contracts won by Chinese, 97 percent of their value went to transport and water sectors (figure 9a). It is striking that the sectoral composition of Chinese-funded projects is completely different: water and roads account for only a small share of this activity, whereas hydro-power, rail, and ICT are much more substantial. One explanation for this is that OECD donors have not devoted significant resources to either hydropower or rail development in recent years. *If Developed world not building new dams or rail roads, = no companies ws to build them, = less experience*

Figure 9: Sectoral and geographic distribution of Chinese-implemented multilateral civil works contracts in sub-Saharan Africa

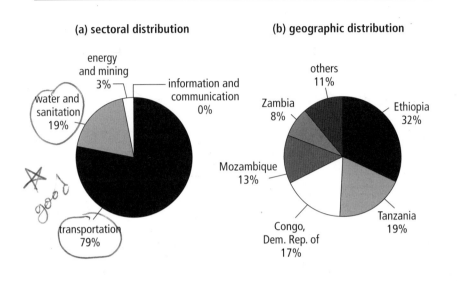

(a) sectoral distribution

energy and mining 3%

water and sanitation 19%

information and communication 0%

transportation 79%

(b) geographic distribution

others 11%

Ethiopia 32%

Zambia 8%

Mozambique 13%

Tanzania 19%

Congo, Dem. Rep. of 17%

Sources: African Development Bank and World Bank Procurement Data (2005–06).

Overall, about 81% of the value of contracts won by Chinese firms under multilateral projects was accounted for by just four countries: Ethiopia, Tanzania, Democratic Republic of Congo, and Mozambique (figure 9b). Once again, this is quite different from the geographic spread under Chinese-funded projects, where more than 70% of the contract value is accounted for by Nigeria, Angola, Ethiopia, and Sudan. This indicates that Chinese contractors have significant presence and experience in a number of countries that have not yet featured prominently in Chinese financing deals.

In summary, the overall picture that emerges is one of a highly successful Chinese contracting sector developing a pre-eminent position in internationally competitive civil works contracts for transport and water projects tendered by multilateral agencies in sub-Saharan Africa. The emergence of Chinese contractors long predates the expansion of Chinese finance for African infrastructure, and may have served as a training ground for the Chinese construction sector in Africa. Nevertheless, the value of multilateral contracts secured by Chinese firms over this period remains much lower that more recent deals based on Chinese finance. What is particularly striking is the contrasting nature of the Chinese contract portfolio based on multilateral finance, versus that based on Chinese finance. Activity funded by multilater-

no oil, but metals

als is focused on roads and water projects in Eastern and Southern Africa. Activity funded by China is focused on hydropower and railways in countries such as Angola, Nigeria, and Sudan. *Oil*

The Natural Resource Side

Sub-Saharan Africa's natural resource exports to China have grown exponentially from just over US$3 billion in 2001 to US$22 billion in 2006. Petroleum accounts for 80 percent of total exports by value over 2001–06 period. The next most important commodities are iron ore and timber (each of which represents 5 percent of total exports), followed by manganese, cobalt, copper, and chromium (each of which represents around 0.5–1 percent of total exports over the same period).

Nevertheless, the bulk of Africa's oil exports continue to go to OECD countries. Over the 2001–06 period, 40 percent of Africa's oil production was exported to the United States, a further 17 percent to Europe, and a further 14 percent to China (figure 10a). China has greater weight as a minerals trading partner, accounting for around 60 percent of Africa's exports of cobalt, 40 percent of exports of iron, and 25–30 percent of exports of chromium, copper, and manganese. China also accounts for 30 percent of the region's timber exports (figure 10b). With the exception of iron, the Chinese share in sub-Saharan Africa exports was increasing at a faster rate for minerals and timber than for oil, over 2001–06 period (figure 10c).

As sub-Saharan Africa's natural resource exports to China have grown, China's relative dependence on sub-Saharan Africa as a supplier of natural resources has also increased (though at a much slower pace). This trend is best illustrated by statistics from the petroleum sector. China currently imports around half of its oil requirements. Africa's share of China's total oil imports has been rising steadily from less than 23 percent in 2001 to 29 percent in 2006 (figure 11a). As a result, sub-Saharan Africa is second only to the Middle East and North Africa in terms of its importance as a supplier of oil imports to China (figure 12a). Within sub-Saharan Africa, Angola is by far the largest supplier, accounting for 50 percent of sub-Saharan Africa's oil exports to China over 2001–06 period (figure 12b). The next most important players are Sudan (18 percent), Republic of Congo (13 percent), and Equatorial Guinea (11 percent). From the perspective of the sub-Saharan African oil producers, China is also a very important client whose imports account for 53 percent of the oil exports of Sudan, and 30 percent of the oil exports of Angola, over 2001–06 period. It is interesting that Nigeria does not feature prominently in Sino-African petroleum trade, although this may change given the volume of recent petroleum deals reported below.

Figure 10: Trends in sub-Saharan African share of exports of selected natural resources going to China and other major trading partners, 2001–06

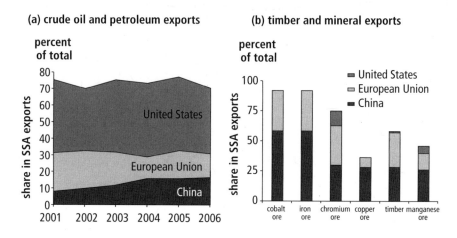

(a) crude oil and petroleum exports

(b) timber and mineral exports

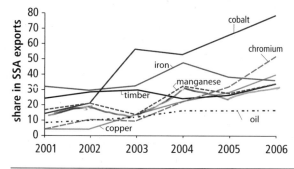

(c) dynamics of the Chinese share in total SSA exports

Source: COMTRADE database by the UNSD, data obtained using WITS software.

Note: SSA = sub-Saharan Africa.

In the case of minerals, China is almost exclusively reliant on sub-Saharan Africa for its cobalt imports, and significantly reliant for manganese (the latter primarily from Gabon, South Africa, and Ghana). Sub-Saharan Africa is also an important supplier of timber (mainly from Gabon, Republic of Congo, and Cameroon) and chromium (mainly from South Africa, Madagascar, and Sudan), accounting for around one-seventh of China's global imports each. However, with respect to China's imports of iron and copper, sub-Saharan Africa is still a relatively small (but growing) contributor (figure 11b).

Comparing Sino-African trading patterns in key natural resources between 2001 and 2006 indicates some shifts in the countries that are supplying China

Figure 11: Sub-Saharan African share of China's imports of selected natural resources, 2001–06

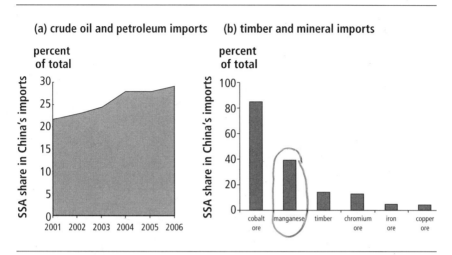

(a) crude oil and petroleum imports   (b) timber and mineral imports

Source: COMTRADE database by the UNSD, data obtained using WITS software.

with specific products (table 8). In the case of petroleum, the relative position of Sudan as an exporter to China has declined. In the case of copper, there has been a major shift away from South Africa and Zambia toward Tanzania and Republic of Congo as the major suppliers. Iron ore imports are also beginning to diversify away from South Africa toward Mozambique and Mauritania. The Democratic Republic of Congo has also increased its share of trade in cobalt ore, while the Republic of Congo has made significant gains in the supply of timber and petroleum.

The pattern of African exports to China has changed substantially over the last few years (figure 13). In 2001, Sudan, Angola, and Equatorial Guinea were the three leading exporters of natural resources to China, with about US$0.5–1 billion of exports each, while South Africa, Gabon, and Republic of Congo were substantially further behind with US$170–300 million each. By 2006, Angola's exports to China had grown to more than US$10 billion. The Republic of Congo has also experienced exponential growth in exports to China, and together with Equatorial Guinea, Sudan, and South Africa is now in the second tier of countries with exports in the range US$1.5–2.5 billion. In addition, countries such as Mauritania, Democratic Republic of Congo, and Chad are also becoming established as Chinese suppliers.

China's oil companies have just recently begun to bid for oil blocks in sub-Saharan Africa, outbidding other international oil companies in a number of

Figure 12: China's oil imports by source, for all regions and for sub-Saharan Africa, 2001–06

(a) by region, percent of total imports

(b) by SSA country, percent of SSA imports

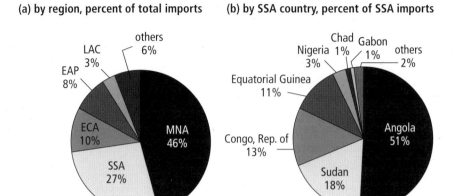

Source: COMTRADE database by the UNSD, data obtained using WITS software.

Note: EAP = East Asia and Pacific; ECA = Europe and Central Asia; LAC = Latin America and the Caribbean; MNA = Middle East and North Africa; SA = South Asia; SSA = sub-Saharan Africa.

recent cases. As a result, they have secured oil exploration and drilling rights in Angola, Chad, Republic of Congo, Côte d'Ivoire, Equatorial Guinea, Ethiopia, Gabon, Kenya, Mali, Mauritania, Niger, Nigeria, São Tomé and Principe, and Sudan. The main players are the major state-owned oil firms: China National Petroleum Corporation (CNPC), Sinopec, and China National Offshore Oil Corporation (CNOOC). In addition to exploration and production, Chinese firms are making major investments in pipeline development, refineries, and terminal capacity, particularly in Nigeria and Sudan.

In countries such as the Democratic Republic of Congo, Guinea, Gabon, Zambia, and Zimbabwe, Chinese companies have secured projects for minerals including copper, iron ore, and bauxite. A wide range of companies have been active in minerals development, including both state-owned enterprises[9] and private business interests.[10] A typical arrangement is for the Chinese

---

[9] Such as China National Overseas Engineering Corporation (COVEC), China Non-Ferrous Metals Mining and Construction Group (NFC), China National Machinery and Equipment Import and Export Corporation (CEMEC), and China Northern Industries Corporation (NORINCO).

[10] Such as Collum Coal Mining, Wambao Resources, Yunnan Copper Group, Xuzhou Huayan, Ningbo Huaneng Kuangyu, and Feza Mining.

Table 8: Shifting patterns of Sino-African trade in selected natural resources (share in total export value of product from Africa to China)

[handwritten note: Significantly China dropped Sudan as oil supplier (!)]

	Top three African exporters to China in 2001			Top three African exporters to China in 2006		
Petroleum	Sudan (37%)	Angola (28%)	Eq. Guinea (17%)	Angola (57%)	Congo, Rep. of (13%)	Eq. Guinea (13%)
Copper ore	S. Africa (96%)	Zambia (4%)	—	S. Africa (26%)	Tanzania (22%)	Congo, Rep. of (13%)
Iron ore	S. Africa (100%)	—	—	S. Africa (98%)	Mozambique (2%)	Mauritania (1%)
Cobalt ore	S. Africa (40%)	Congo, Dem. Rep. of (33%)	Congo, Rep. of (22%)	Congo, Dem. Rep. of (73%)	Congo, Rep. of (18%)	S. Africa (8%)
Manganese ore	Ghana (52%)	Gabon (41%)	S. Africa (3%)	Gabon (50%)	S. Africa (35%)	Ghana (14%)
Timber	Gabon (56%)	Eq. Guinea (21%)	Liberia (8%)	Gabon (44%)	Congo, Rep. of (16%)	Cameroon (15%)
Chromium ore	S. Africa (73%)	Madagascar (27%)	—	S. Africa (91%)	Madagascar (5%)	Sudan (4%)

Source: COMTRADE database by the UNSD, data obtained using WITS software.

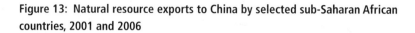

Figure 13: Natural resource exports to China by selected sub-Saharan African countries, 2001 and 2006

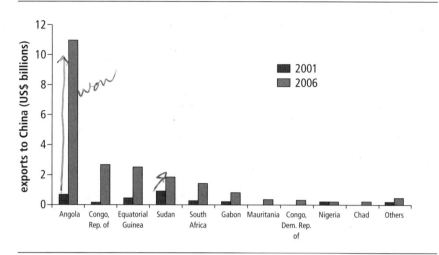

Source: COMTRADE database by the UNSD, data obtained using WITS software.

investor (whether private or state owned) to form a joint venture with the local African state-owned mining enterprise, as has taken place for example in Democratic Republic of Congo, Gabon, and Zambia.[11]

To understand this trend better, a parallel projects database was prepared based on the Factiva data tool using international press sources, to identify natural resource projects in Africa where China had secured some kind of equity stake. The database records around 100 natural resource projects with Chinese involvement. As with the infrastructure projects reported above, project information was taken from international press reports and subsequently validated from official Chinese Web sites using the same methodology already described. The data presented below include only projects that could be validated from Chinese sources. Unfortunately, the value of the associated investment commitments is not given for all of the reported projects. Although we were able to confirm existence of 80 natural resources projects, the investment commitments were available and confirmed in only 27 cases. There-

---

[11] The respective African counterparts being MKM in Democratic Republic of Congo, Industrial and Commercial Mines Company of Gabon (CICMG), and Zambia Consolidated Copper Mine (ZCCM).

fore the figures given below are a likely lower bound on the total value. A detailed tabulation of Chinese-funded natural resource projects by country can be found in annex 5.

The database documents a rapidly rising trend in Chinese commitments to African natural resource development, with deals in excess of US$9 billion reported in 2006, compared with a value of around US$194 million in the year 2005. No investment commitments could be confirmed in earlier years. The 2007 deals for which financing information was available amounted to US$1.3 billion. Most of the total commitments were directed at natural resource development and hence could be considered FDI. Some of it was paid directly to governments largely in the form of one-time royalties or "signature bonuses" required to secure oil exploration and production licenses. These figures are high in relation to historical levels of Chinese FDI reported for Africa, with the most recent figures indicating annual flows of US$400 million for 2004–05, although recent research highlights significant limitation in capturing oil sector FDI in official statistics (Aukut and Goldstein 2007). Given that the projects database reports commitments, while FDI relates to actual disbursements, a significant lag could be expected. Nevertheless, based on these reports a substantial increase in Chinese FDI to Africa can be predicted for the coming years.

Some 71 percent of at least US$10.6 billion Chinese commitments to the natural resources sector relate to petroleum, with the balance going to minerals—mainly copper and chromium, but also cobalt, iron, bauxite, manganese, coal, nickel, titanium, and uranium (table 9). Although at least 26 countries have received some investment in natural resource development, Nigeria and Angola stand out as by far the largest recipients of natural resource investment, predominantly in petroleum. Despite the inability to confirm putative US$1.3 billion of commitments to exploration and transportation of Sudanese oil, the quantity of the recorded natural resources projects in Sudan points to its strategic importance for China. Box 2 below provides further details of the nature of Chinese involvement in the oil sectors of each of these three oil-rich countries. China has also been taking an interest in countries that are just beginning to identify and exploit new hydrocarbon resources. For example, in 2006, CNOOC purchased 50 percent interest in oil block covering seven sedimentary basins in Chad, from Canadian producer EnCana. Subsequently, CNOOC made its first commercial discovery of oil in Chad in mid 2007. In addition, Chinese petroleum companies have exploration activities underway in a number of countries not yet considered to be oil producers, such as Central African Republic, Ethiopia, Liberia, Madagascar, and Somalia.

Nevertheless, this vigorous growth of natural resource trade between China and Africa, takes place from a very low base. The fact remains that China's oil companies are relative latecomers to petroleum exploration and production in Africa. Thus, the US$7.5 billion of Chinese oil sector investments recorded above are less than a tenth of the US$168 billion that other international oil companies have already invested in the region (Downs 2007).

South Africa is currently in the first place as a recipient of natural resource finance due to major investments related to solid minerals, mainly chromium, cobalt, iron, gold and nickel. However, China has also shown a growing interest in the mining belt of central-southern Africa, comprising Zambia, Tanzania, and Mozambique. This area is well endowed with copper, iron, gold, manganese, and other base metals. Of these three countries, Zambia has the most advanced level of Chinese engagement. In Zambia, China has secured direct equity interests in copper, coal, and manganese. The purchase of an 85 percent stake of Chambishi copper mine for about US$20 million in 1998 was one of China's earliest overseas mining investments. After its reopening in 2003, the mine has seen continuous inflow of more than US$200 million of new investment, including construction of the smelter plants. The mine's production capacity is expected to reach 150,000 tons of copper per year in 2008. In coal, Chinese Collum Mine at the old Nkandabbwe Mine in Sinazongwe district started production in 2003 and recorded an output of 20,000 tons in 2004. In 2005, a private Chinese firm purchased a manganese mine with proven deposit of 4 million tons in Zambia's old industrial town of Kabwe. The processing of manganese started in 2007. In 2006, around 27 percent of Zambia's exports of copper were destined for China, compared to 100 percent of manganese.[12]

Comparing table 9 on the pattern of current Chinese natural resource investments with table 8 indicating the current pattern of Chinese natural resource imports from Africa provides some pointers as to the future direction of trade flows. Whereas table 8 above indicated that Nigeria is not currently a major supplier of oil to China, the new Chinese commitments to petroleum sector development in Nigeria reported in this section suggest that Nigeria's volume of oil exports to China is set to increase. The same could be said of Gabon, which today does not feature as an exporter of iron ore to China, but which is receiving a substantial investment in the mining sector, particularly into the Belinga iron ore reserve, capable of producing 15 million tons per year. In many cases, the exact value of the investment could not be ascer-

---

[12] COMTRADE database by the United Nations Statistics Division (UNSD), data obtained using WITS software.

Table 9: Chinese investment commitments in natural resource sector in sub-Saharan Africa, 2001–07 (US$ millions)

	Oil	Chromium	Copper	Iron	Bauxite	Coal	Manganese	Multiple	Other minerals	Total
Angola	2,400	0	0	0	0	0	0	0	0	2,400
Central African Republic	—	0	0	0	0	0	0	0	0	—
Chad	>203	0	0	0	0	0	0	0	0	>203
Congo, Dem. Rep. of	—	0	—	0	0	0	0	>370[a]	—	>370
Congo, Rep. of	—	0	0	0	0	0	0	0	0	—
Côte d'Ivoire	—	0	0	0	0	0	—	0	0	—
Equatorial Guinea	—	0	0	0	0	0	0	0	0	—
Eritrea	0	0	—	0	0	0	0	60[b]	—	>60
Gabon	—	0	0	—	0	0	2	0	—	>2
Guinea	0	0	0	0	63	0	0	0	—	>63
Kenya	—	0	0	0	0	0	0	0	24	>24
Liberia	—	0	0	0	0	0	0	0	0	—
Madagascar	103	0	0	0	0	0	0	0	0	103
Mali	—	0	0	0	0	0	0	0	0	—
Mauritania	>9	0	0	0	0	0	0	0	0	>9
Mozambique	—	0	0	0	0	0	0	0	—	—
Multiple countries	0	0	0	0	0	0	0	783[c]	0	783
Namibia	0	0	—	0	0	0	0	0	0	—
Niger	—	0	0	0	0	0	0	0	—	—
Nigeria	>4,762	0	0	0	0	0	0	300[d]	19	>5,081

(continued)

Table 9: *continued*

	Oil	Chromium	Copper	Iron	Bauxite	Coal	Manganese	Multiple	Other minerals	Total
São Tomé and Príncipe	—	0	0	0	0	0	0	0	0	—
Somalia	—	0	0	0	0	0	0	0	0	—
South Africa	0	537	0	—	0	0	0	510[e]	—	>1,047
Sudan	—	0	0	—	0	0	0	0	4	>4
Tanzania	0	0	0	0	0	—	0	0	0	—
Zambia	0	0	220	0	0	—	—	0	25	>245
Zimbabwe	0	200	—	0	0	—	0	0	0	>200
Total	>7,476	>737	>220	—	63	—	>2	>2,023	>71	>10,591

Source: World Bank–PPIAF Chinese Projects Database (2008).

Note: " — " = project was reported but that the value of the commitment was not given.

a. Copper and cobalt

b. Copper and gold

c. Purchase of shareholding in Anglo-American group with operations in platinum, diamonds, coal, base metals, and ferrous metals in Botswana, Namibia, South Africa, and Tanzania

d. Oil and solid minerals

e. Iron and chromium, cobalt and nickel.

Figure 14: Country shares of Chinese natural resource investment and finance commitments into power and transport in sub-Saharan Africa, 2001–07

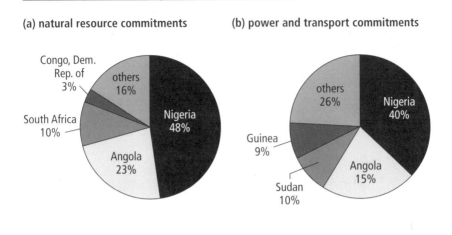

(a) natural resource commitments   (b) power and transport commitments

Source: World Bank–PPIAF Chinese Projects Database (2008).

tained. Thus, for example, Chinese oil sector investment of unknown magnitude has been reported in countries as diverse as Côte d'Ivoire, Ethiopia, Gabon, Equatorial Guinea, Kenya, Liberia, and Mali.

Overall, there is some correspondence between countries with large Chinese natural resource investments and those with large Chinese infrastructure financing into power and transport (figure 14). One explanation for this lies in the fact that infrastructure is often the bottleneck that prevents African countries from realizing their full potential as natural resource exporters. As a result, FDI in the natural resource sector is sometimes packaged with official finance for infrastructure needed to facilitate development and export. This may include power for processing, and rail and port facilities for outward transportation. Some concrete examples recorded by the database are provided in table 10 below.

However, these deals only account for US$1.6 billion, or for 10 percent of US$16 billion total Chinese infrastructure finance reported in this study. While a large share of Chinese infrastructure finance goes to major natural resource exporters, and a certain amount of that goes on projects that facilitate natural resource development, the bulk of Chinese infrastructure finance is targeted toward projects that meet the country's broader development needs.

Table 10: Chinese-financed infrastructure projects linked to Chinese natural resource development projects

Country	Year of commitment	Status at end of 2007	Link to natural resource development	Project description	Chinese financing commitments (US$ millions)
Botswana	2006	Proposed	To provide means of transportation of coal to China from landlocked Botswana via Namibian ports	Construction of the Trans-Kgalagadi railway that would link Botswana with Namibia	Not available
Gabon	2006	Agreement	Provides means of transportation for the iron ore output from the Belinga Mine	Belinga iron ore project. Includes construction of Poubara hydropower dam, Belinga-Santa Clara railway, and the deep-water port at Santa Clara, with total projects cost of US$3 billion.	Not available
Guinea	2006	Under reconsideration	Power needed to process bauxite associated with China's mining interests	Construction of Souapiti Dam hydropower 750 MW project	1,000
Mauritania	2007	Agreement	Facilitates phosphate mining from the reserves near the town of Bofal, close to Senegal's border	Construction of 430 km railway from Nouakchott to Bofal	620
Total					1,620

Source: World Bank–PPIAF Chinese Projects Database (2008).

BOX 2

Chinese involvement in petroleum sector development in Nigeria, Angola, and Sudan

Nigeria: A rapidly growing engagement

Since 2004, Chinese petroleum companies have acquired various interests in Nigerian oil production. This began when Sinopec won an initial oil exploration contract for blocks 64 and 66 of the Chad Basin. In 2006, both China National Oil Corporation (CNOOC) and China National Petroleum Corporation (CNPC) won substantial interests in Nigerian oil exploration.

CNOOC purchased 45 percent of block ML130 in the Niger Delta, with reserve estimates of 600 million barrels covering about 500 square miles of Akpo Oilfield and other discoveries. The total deal offered by CNOCC was worth US$2.7 billion.

Just several months later, CNPC completed the acquisition of a 51 percent stake in the Kaduna refinery for a total consideration of US$2 billion. The refinery was designed to refine 110,000 barrels of oil a day, yet due to lack of maintenance, its actual refinery capacity was only 70 percent of that capacity. Together with this deal, CNPC received the license for four oil blocks—OPL 471, 721, 732, and 298. As a result of these deals, Chinese state-owned oil companies committed to invest around US$5 billion in the country's petroleum industry.

Angola: A joint venture between state-owned enterprises

The China Petroleum and Chemical Corporation (SINOPEC) and Angola National Oil Corporation (Sonangol) signed a contract for the establishment of a joint venture, Sonangol Sinopec International (SSI), to exploit crude oil in Angola's three offshore oil fields in 2006. Sinopec held a 75 percent share, while Sonangol of Angola had the remaining 25 percent. SINOPEC, China's biggest oil refinement corporation, was to contribute about US$2.4 billion, including government signature bonuses of US$2.2 billion and US$200 million investment in social projects. SSI won a 27.5 percent stake in block 17, a 40 percent stake in block 18, and a 20 percent working interest in block 15. With block 15 holding approximately 1.5 billion barrels of oil reserves, block 17 holding 1 billion barrels, and block 18 holding 700 million barrels, it was estimated that the three blocks would bring Sinopec around 100,000 barrels of oil output per day.

(continued)

BOX 2

continued

SSI also announced plans to develop a US$3 billion refinery in Lobito with maximum capacity of 240,000 barrels per day, under the project known as Sonaref. However, the negotiations around Sonaref collapsed and the project was canceled in 2007. Angola's current oil refinery capacity is around 39,000 barrels per day.

Sudan: First major African oil experience

During 2001–07, the database recorded six confirmed oil-related projects in Sudan. However, none of the total recorded commitments for Sudan amounting to some US$645 million was confirmed by Chinese sources. The database also has information on another six unconfirmed oil projects, amounting to additional US$789 million of possible finance commitments.

Project sponsorship in Sudan has taken the form of complex multinational consortia with other emerging financiers. In most cases, the leading minority stake goes to CNPC, which has formed a joint venture with the Sudanese government to bid for blocks. Other members of the consortium typically include Petronas of Malaysia, and the Al Thani Corporation of the United Arab Emirates, with Sinopec of China sometimes participating with a small stake. Moreover, in 2005, Indian and Chinese companies collaborated on an African oil project for the first time through the Greater Nile Petroleum Operating Company (GNPOC)—a joint venture of CNPC (40 percent) and ONGC Vindesh (25 percent)—which won the rights to the Heglig and Unity fields (blocks 1, 2, and 4).

Source: Authors.

Oil exploration deals in Sudan have not entailed the payment of major royalty payments to the government, but rather the entire investment commitments in the industry to date have gone directly into exploration and construction of supporting pipeline and refinery infrastructure. Furthermore, China has provided additional finance to support development of oil-related infrastructure, including pipelines, pumping facilities, and export terminals all related to exploitation of the Melut Basin oil field. Similarly, pipelines and oil terminals are being constructed to facilitate the export of oil from

Blocks 3, 6, and 7. There have also been significant investments in expanding the capacity of the Khartoum oil refinery. Exploration and production activities are so far taking place in blocks 1, 2, 3, 4, 7, and 15.

6.

THE FINANCING PERSPECTIVE

Loans from the China Export-Import (Ex-Im) Bank account for the vast majority—92 percent—of the recorded Chinese infrastructure finance commitments in sub-Saharan Africa in 2001–07 (figure 15a). Another category is "Chinese government unspecified" financing, which accounts for 3 percent of the total, and may indicate funding directly from the executive branch of government, likely to be the Ministry of Commerce. More recently, a number of projects have been funded by the China-Africa Development Fund established by the China Development Bank (CDB). This follows public announcements of CDB's intention to rapidly expand its overseas portfolio.[13] CDB is China's major domestic development bank and the world's largest development bank as measured by assets. Fifty percent of the recorded commitments are loans, and a further 44 percent take the form of export credits (figure 15b).

Given the pre-eminence of the China Ex-Im Bank, this section analyzes the bank's practices in greater detail, and brings together the limited information available on loan financing terms. It also considers the financial impact of Chinese loans on the overall indebtedness of the African countries involved.

The Role of China Ex-Im Bank

As a state policy bank founded in 1994, China Ex-Im's official mission is to carry out state industrial policies, foreign economic and trade policies, and diplomatic policies. While state banks such as CDB specialize in domestic development, the Ex-Im Bank was set up to focus on overseas projects. The

---

[13] Reported in the *Financial Times of London* (December 6, 2006).

Figure 15: Chinese infrastructure finance commitments in sub-Saharan Africa by source and type, 2001–07

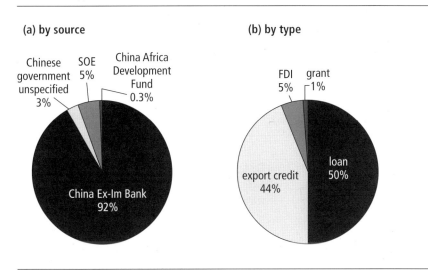

(a) by source

Chinese government unspecified 3%
SOE 5%
China Africa Development Fund 0.3%
China Ex-Im Bank 92%

(b) by type

FDI 5%
grant 1%
loan 50%
export credit 44%

Source: World Bank–PPIAF Chinese Projects Database (2008).

Ex-Im Bank offers several products, the most important of which are export buyers' and sellers' credits, international guarantees, on-loaned funds extended by foreign governments and financial institutions, as well as concessional and nonconcessional loans for overseas construction and investment projects. The Ex-Im Bank is the only Chinese institution that is empowered to provide concessional lending to overseas projects.

Concessional loans require a sovereign guarantee, and where the government's creditworthiness may be an issue, the loans are sometimes backed by natural resources. In the case of export buyers' credits, sovereign guarantees are also needed in most cases; however, local banks with a good record of creditworthiness or local branches of internationally recognized banks may also be able to provide acceptable guarantees under some circumstances.

As a state policy bank handling bilateral aid, details on much of the lending activities of the Ex-Im Bank are not made public. While the annual reports of the bank do disclose the total amounts of export buyers' and sellers' credits per year, it is not broken down by specific agreements. The section on concessional lending activities does not reveal the level of disbursements.

However, according to the report, "During the 'Tenth Five-Year Plan' period (2001–05), the Bank signed 78 concessional loan projects for foreign countries, with the approved loans increasing by 35 percent on an annual basis; the outstanding loans by 28 percent; and the accumulated disbursements by 22 percent. The prioritization for concessional loans typically goes to sectors closely related to the economic development of the recipient countries, such as electric power, transportation and telecommunication."

The available information provided by the China Ex-Im Bank makes clear that the scale of its operations is increasing (figure 16). According to Moss and Rose (2006), the China Ex-Im Bank may now be one of the largest export credit agencies in the world, with primary commercial operations in 2005 greater than Organisation for Economic Co-operation and Development (OECD) Ex-Im Banks such as those in the United States, Japan, and the United Kingdom. Because China is not an OECD member, it has no obligation to follow OECD reporting requirements. Since China does not have a separate bilateral donor institution, the China Ex-Im Bank has largely assumed this role, further differentiating it from OECD Ex-Im Banks.

By providing preferred lines of credit to Chinese state-owned enterprises and foreign governments wishing to purchase Chinese-made goods, the China Ex-Im Bank supports the overseas expansion of Chinese firms in line with the country's "Go Global" strategy, to increase the productivity and competitiveness of these enterprises.

Figure 16: Commitments by China Ex-Im Bank, 2001–06

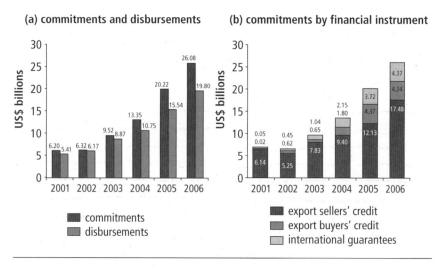

(a) commitments and disbursements

(b) commitments by financial instrument

Source: China Ex-Im Bank (2007).

In the case of concessional loans, there is a requirement that a Chinese enterprise be selected as the contractor or exporter. Moreover, no less than 50 percent of the equipment, materials, services, or technology needed to implement the project should be secured from China. *Ghana's Buses*

Concessional loans are founded on two legal agreements. The first is an Intergovernmental Framework Agreement signed by both governments indicating the purpose, amount, maturity, and interest rate of the facility. The second is a loan agreement signed by the China Ex-Im Bank and the borrower within that framework. Relatively little is known about the terms of the China Ex-Im Bank's concessional loans. However, the range of interest rates offered by the bank across all its products is 2–7 percent, in addition to some direct grants. Interest rates for specific deals are determined on the basis of a matrix that takes both the economic situation and the commercial viability of the project into account. *good rates*

The China Ex-Im Bank was originally created with a mandate to cover costs, without necessarily making a profit; as a result in the past it has done little more than to break even. In recent years there is a growing interest in more commercially oriented lending. Initially, the China Ex-Im Bank only provided loans to state-owned enterprises. However, more recently it has broadened its range of clients to include private Chinese enterprises, and foreign enterprises active in China. *not profit driven*

The China Ex-Im Bank is making increasing use of a deal structure—known as "Angola mode" or "resources for infrastructure"—whereby repayment of the loan for infrastructure development is made in terms of natural resources (for example, oil). This approach is by no means novel or unique, but follows a long history of natural resource-based transactions in the oil industry (Johnston 1994). Indeed, its use in Angola by Western corporations in the earlier years of this century has also been widely documented (HRW 2001).

The Angola mode is increasingly being used by the China Ex-Im Bank for countries that cannot provide adequate financial guarantees to back their loan commitments. Under this arrangement, the money is never directly transferred to the government (as illustrated in figure 17). Instead, a framework agreement is signed with the government covering a certain program of infrastructure investments. These are contracted to a Chinese construction firm. At the same time, a Chinese petroleum company is awarded rights to begin production. The government of the beneficiary country instructs the Chinese contractor to undertake infrastructure works, supported by a credit from China Ex-Im Bank. Repayment is in the form of oil produced directly by the Chinese petroleum company. The organization of the deal is relatively complex owing

Angola Mode explanation

Figure 17: Structure of "Angola mode" arrangement

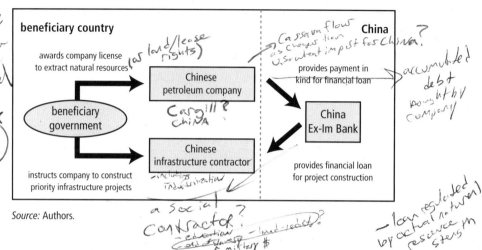

Source: Authors.

to the need to coordinate with the two Chinese firms involved, each of which must carry out its own due diligence. The arrangement allows countries with abundant resources but limited creditworthiness to package the exploitation of natural resources with the development of infrastructure assets.

The financial terms of Angola mode are particularly difficult to pinpoint, given that they depend to a significant extent on the implicit price agreed upon for the commodity traded, and its relation to current and future market prices, so that any discount provided with respect to the future price of oil effectively contributes to a hardening of lending terms (or vice versa). Using the Angola mode method of finance, China is able to gain physical security over oil resources, normally at a slightly discounted price. Although the detailed terms of these Chinese oil-backed loans are not known, according to oil industry specialists at the World Bank the wider experience with deals of this kind suggests that they do not typically entail fixing the price of oil over the term of the loan. In fact, as oil prices rise and fall over the period, the term of the loan is usually adjusted accordingly; for example, a shortening of the repayment period as the price of oil rises. In this sense, credit deals tied to repayment in oil are not really a hedge against the future price of oil, but rather provide a way of securing a steady supply into the medium term.

A growing number of such resource-backed financing schemes were identified in the infrastructure projects database created for this paper. Table 11 documents eight deals totaling more than US$3 billion. The first reported example of the arrangement was a relatively small deal in the Republic of

Table 11: Chinese-financed infrastructure projects backed by natural resources, 2001–07

Country	Year of commitment	Status at the end of 2007	Natural resource to be received in payment	Project description	Total Chinese financing (US$ millions)
Congo, Rep. of	2001	Under construction	Oil	Congo River Dam. Backed by crude oil guarantees.	280
Sudan	2001	Completed	Oil	Construction of the El-Gaili (Al Jaily) Power Plant, first two phases with Sudan's oil serving as collateral for the loans.	128
Angola	2004	Completed	Oil	Oil-backed loan to repair damaged infrastructure bombed in the country's civil war (power, transport, ICT, and water portion). China to receive 10,000 barrels of oil per day.	1,020
Nigeria	2005	Under construction	Oil	Construction of gas turbine power plant at Papalanto. PetroChina secured by a deal to purchase 30,000 barrels of crude oil a day from the Nigerian National Petroleum Corporation for a period of one year, renewable.	298
Guinea	2006	Under reconsideration	Bauxite	Souapiti Dam project. Reportedly linked to mining (bauxite) revenues.	1,000
Gabon	2006	Agreement	Iron	Bélinga iron ore reserve. Loan is to be repaid via sales of iron ore to China.	Not available
Zimbabwe	2006	Agreement, possibly not materialized	Chromium	Construction of new coal mines and three thermal power stations in Dande, in the Zambezi valley on the Zambian border. In exchange, Zimbabwe was to provide China with chromium.	Not available
Ghana	2007	Under construction	Cocoa	Bui Dam hydropower project. Part of the loan will be repaid in cocoa exports to China.	562
Total					3,287

Source: World Bank–PPIAF Chinese Projects Database (2008).

Handwritten annotations: "at discount price?"; "Shut down due to mistrust or democratic swing?"

Congo in 2001. However, since the landmark oil-backed deal with Angola in 2004, the mechanism has become more popular, and the resources used to back deals have diversified to include bauxite, chromium, iron ore, and even cocoa. The common state ownership of most of the major oil and infrastructure corporations makes it easier to coordinate this kind of bundled multisectoral deal.

Financing Terms

As noted above, there is no public information available as to the financial terms offered by the China Ex-Im Bank on its concessional financing deals. It was, however, possible to identify some of the projects that were financed by grants from the Ministry of Commerce, because these are published on an official Web site for the benefit of prospective contractors (table 12). Although the exact financial value of each project was not always available, in general these appear to have been small projects, of little more than US$10 million on average. Many of them take place in smaller countries, such as Burundi, Cape Verde, Comoros, and Rwanda. Moreover, the projects themselves relate either to rehabilitation of power plants or construction of prestige transport infrastructure projects (airports, bridges, bypasses).

All members of the World Bank who borrow from the International Development Association or the International Bank for Reconstruction and Development are required to report the value and financial terms of their external debt (including public, publicly guaranteed, and private nonguaranteed debt) to the World Bank's Debtor Reporting System (DRS), so that their overall creditworthiness can be assessed. From the DRS it is difficult to trace specific projects, because only very general descriptions of loan purpose are typically included. Nevertheless, it is possible to obtain an overall indication of the average financial terms on Chinese loans to specific countries. These may or may not correspond to the specific infrastructure projects recorded in the project database developed for this report. However, given that infrastructure is a central focus of Chinese lending to sub-Saharan Africa, the overlap is likely to be quite large. Unfortunately, only very partial DRS data for 2006 (the year with the highest volumes of Chinese finance to date) were available at the time of this writing.

The International Development Association applies a grant element calculation to permit standardized comparison of financial terms across deals and to establish whether or not the financial terms can be deemed concessional. For any particular set of financial terms (including interest rate, grace period, and repayment period) the calculator determines the equivalent percentage grant component that would have to be applied to a standard loan at market

Table 12: Chinese grant-financed infrastructure projects in sub-Saharan Africa, 2004–07

[handwritten: Gifts as loans so concessional, that partly a gift]

Country	Year of commitment	Sector	Project description	Chinese finance (US$ m)
Cape Verde	2004	Power	Reconstruction of Palião Dam	—
Comoros	2004	Transport	Renovation of Prince Said Ibraim International Airport	7
Gúinea	2004	Power	Rehabilitation of Ginkang & Tinkisso hydropower plants	2
Nigeria	2004	Water	Construction of 598 water schemes for 19 states	—
Rwanda	2004	Transport	Construction of a 2.6 km road as part of Kigali ring road	—
Burundi	2005	Power	Rehabilitation of Gikonge & Ruvyironza hydroplants	—
Ethiopia	2006	Transport	Construction of Gotera intersection bridge in Addis	13
Kenya	2006	Transport	Rehabilitation of link road to Kenyatta International Airport	28
Chad	2007	Transport	Rehabilitation of six roads in N'Djamena	—
Gabon	2007	Transport	Rehabilitation of 17 roads in Gabon (10 km total)	—
Kenya	2007	Transport	Construction of roads in Nairobi	23
Lesotho	2007	ICT	Establishment of television systems in five cities	—
Mali	2007	Transport	Construction of the "Third" bridge in Bamako	—
Niger	2007	Transport	Construction of bridge over River Niger in Niamey	30
Tanzania	2007	Water	Rehabilitation/extension of water system in Chalinze	—
Togo	2007	Power	Construction of generating unit for Tomegbe	—

Source: China, Ministry of Commerce 2007.

[handwritten notes at bottom: Central – long centre – converge — Bus + Tram + TQ interchange + KNM area as extension of KNM to airport. Could also be reconfiguring Accra's transport infrastructure for Bus Rapid Transit + freeway system beyond of freeway system Kwame Nkrumah Motorway]

The Financing Perspective | 59

terms to achieve the same financial profile as that offered by the loan in question. It is important to recall that in the specific case of the Angola mode deals cited in table 11 above, these financial terms do not give the full picture because they fail to quantify the impact of any discount offered on the future price of natural resources.

According to the OECD-DAC (Development Assistance Committee) definition, official credits with an implicit grant element of at least 25 percent can be regarded as official development assistance (ODA).[14] Based on this definition, Chinese lending on average would contain a grant element of about 36 percent. However, given today's low interest rate environment, the major disadvantage of the ODA-DAC methodology, which uses a fixed 10 percent discount rate, is that it overestimates the concessionality of a loan. For comparative purposes, the results obtained using the OECD-DAC definition are reported in all the tables and figures below. However, the discussion centers on the OECD-ECA definition, defined below, which is now more widely used for the purposes of calculating debt sustainability.

The OECD-ECA (Export Credit Agreement) defines a loan as concessional when it has a grant element of 35 percent or more using regularly updated currency-specific commercial interest reference rates. This definition has been adopted both by the International Monetary Fund (IMF) and the World Bank. As a point of reference, using this definition, IDA credits incorporate a grant element of about 70 percent, and are based on zero interest (but a 0.75 percent service charge), a 10- year grace period and a 40-year repayment term.[15]

Table 13 presents the average terms on all Chinese lending to various African countries in recent years, including both infrastructure and other types of loans. On average, the Chinese loans offer an interest rate of 3.1 percent, a grace period of 4 years, and a maturity of 13 years. Overall, this represents a grant element of around 18 percent based on the OECD-ECA definition of concessionality. Nevertheless, the variation around all of these parameters is considerable across countries; thus interest rates range from 1 to 6 percent, grace periods from 2 to 10 years, maturities between 5 and 25 years, and overall grant elements between 0 and 55 percent, so that a subset of the loans to lie above the concessionality threshold.

At the same time, the terms for individual countries that received multiple loans over a number of different years are generally very consistent (figure 18a). The relationship between financial terms and gross national income (GNI) per capita is very weak (figure 18b). While some of the most concessional terms (around 55 percent) go to the poorest countries such as Ethiopia

---

[14] Credits are also required to be concessional in nature to be regarded as ODA.
[15] IDA homepage.

Table 13: Average terms of all Chinese official loans to various sub-Saharan African countries, 2002–06

Year	Country	Chinese finance (US$ m)	Interest rate (%)	Grace period (yrs)	Financing term (yrs)	Grant element (OECD-DAC) (%)	Grant element (OECD-ECA) (%)
2002	Cape Verde	1.2	3.0	10.1	14.1	48	25
	Gabon	7.6	1.0	2.0	8.5	34	22
	Gambia, The	25.5	4.0	8.4	24.4	45	27
	Mauritius	12.1	4.0	4.8	12.3	32	13
	Nigeria	377.0	4.8	3.9	10.9	26	6
	Sudan	57.7	4.3	3.5	11.1	28	10
	Zimbabwe	27.0	6.4	1.3	5.8	10	0
2003	Botswana	29.7	3.2	5.1	14.9	41	20
	Sudan	33.8	5.1	1.2	6.1	13	3
	Swaziland	10.0	3.3	3.1	19.6	42	25
	Zimbabwe	69.0	6.1	0.4	5.3	10	0
2004	Angola	2,000.0	1.2	3.5	15.5	50	37
	Benin	2.4	1.0	10.1	20.1	68	53
	Ethiopia	13.0	1.0	11.2	20.2	69	55
	Sudan	74.7	3.7	2.7	8.8	25	11
2005	Mauritania	136.0	3.0	3.4	18.9	43	27
	Seychelles	1.0	2.0	4.2	9.7	38	22
	Sudan	9.0	4.0	2.8	6.8	21	8
	Zimbabwe	6.6	6.4	0.7	4.7	8	0
2006	Botswana	28.7	3.0	5.4	15.3	41	26
	Ghana	30.0	2.0	5.0	20.0	53	39
	Nigeria	200.0	3.0	2.2	8.7	27	13
	Sudan	3.5	4.0	1.6	4.6	15	5
	Zimbabwe	200.0	6.1	0.4	1.9	4	0

Source: World Bank's Debtor Reporting System, 2006.

Note: In calculating the OECD-ECA grant element we use the average financing terms for each country or group to calculate the grant element, which may lead to some under- or overestimation. In addition, the following assumptions are made: (a) the commitment is fully disbursed; (b) the number of repayments per annum is twice; (c) repayment is on an equal principal repayment basis; (d) interest rates are fixed; (e) the discount rate is the relevant and latest available Commercial Interest Reference Rate (CIRR) for the U.S. dollar plus the relevant margin as set out under the OECD-ECA definition and consistent with the IMF Poverty Reduction and Growth Facility (PRGF) Performance Criteria; and (f) where the information on maturity is not available, 10-year maturity is assumed. In calculating the OECD-DAC grant element the same assumptions (a) through (d) are made, while on point (e) the discount rate is assumed to take the fixed value of 10 percent used in OECD-DAC calculations. The calculation of grant element does not take into account, if any, fees, commitment charges, procurement conditions and so on as such information is unavailable.

Figure 18: Average grant element of Chinese lending to selected sub-Saharan African countries, 2002–06

(a) by country   (b) against GNI pc

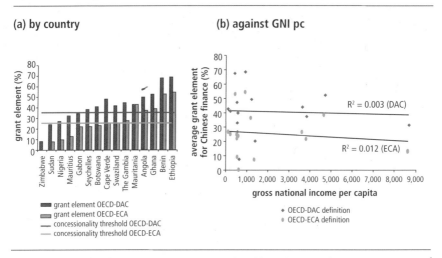

Sources: World Bank's, Debtor Reporting System, 2006 and World Development Indicators.

and Benin, other countries in a similar income bracket receive less favorable terms. Moreover, middle-income countries such as Botswana, Cape Verde and Gabon still receive comparatively large grant elements of 20–25 percent. Loans to Zimbabwe were on substantially harder terms than those for any other country. *due to unreliable nature*

Using the same DRS source, table 14 compares Chinese financing terms for sub-Saharan Africa and other developing countries with those offered by other creditors. The evidence shows that on average African countries receive more favorable borrowing terms than other developing nations. Based on the OECD-ECA definition of concessionality, the overall average grant element for a sub-Saharan Africa from all creditors is 33 percent versus 14 percent for other developing countries. This difference is almost entirely driven by much more favorable terms from official creditors, which lend to sub-Saharan Africa at a grant element of 54 percent versus 34 percent for developing countries as a whole. Rates offered by Chinese creditors to sub-Saharan Africa amount to a grant element of around 18 percent based on this definition.

Country Indebtedness

The growing volume of Chinese debt finance being made available to African countries comes in the wake of increased grant provision and major debt relief efforts. As a result of bilateral (Paris Club) and multilateral (Heavily Indebted Poor Countries [HIPC] and Multilateral Debt Relief Initiative

Table 14: Financing terms offered by China and other creditors to sub-Saharan Africa and all developing countries, 2002–06

Type of creditor	Interest rates (%)	Grace period (yrs)	Financing term (yrs)	Grant element (OECD-DAC) (%)	Grant element (OECD-ECA) (%)
All developing countries					
All creditors	4.8	7.4	15.2	30	14
Official creditors only	2.8	5.9	22.2	49	34
Private creditors	6.0	8.3	10.9	19	0
Sub-Saharan Africa					
All creditors	2.9	5.9	22.3	45	33
Official creditors only	1.7	7.7	32.9	66	54
Private creditors	4.7	3.4	7.2	17	5
Chinese creditors only	3.1	3.6	13.2	36	18

Source: World Bank, Debtor Reporting System (2006).

Notes: For methodology underlying grant element calculation, see previous table.

[MDRI] initiatives, the sub-Saharan African countries covered in this study were forgiven a total of US$89 billion of bilateral and multilateral debt up to 2007, much of it concessional in nature. China itself has also provided a significant amount of debt relief to African countries totaling at least US$780 million since the year 2000. The major beneficiaries have been Zambia, Ethiopia, Angola, Tanzania, Republic of Congo, Uganda, Ghana and Guinea.

The reduced indebtedness of African countries that benefited from this debt relief has created significant fiscal space allowing these countries to borrow again to finance much needed investments. Debt relief was granted on the understanding that future indebtedness would be carefully monitored to ensure its macroeconomic sustainability.

To provide a very approximate sense of the materiality of potential African indebtedness to China under the recent agreements documented above, table 15 provides a country-by-country comparison of the face value of recent OECD debt relief against new financial commitments to China.[16] The ratio of

---

[16] Given widespread default, the market value of the debt that was forgiven would have been substantially below the face value reported here.

Table 15: Comparison of debt relief with Chinese loan commitments, 2000–07 (US$ millions except where otherwise specified)

Country	Paris Club (since 2000) (A)	HIPC (IDA) (B)	MDRI (IDA) (C)	Total debt relief (A+B+C)	Chinese infra-structure finance (D)	Chinese finance over Western debt relief (%) (D)/(A+B+C)
Angola	0	0	0	0	3,200	n.a.
Burundi	90	1,465	0	1,555	8	1
Cameroon	1,990	4,917	1,266	8,173	24	0
Central African Republic	0	0	0	0	67	n.a.
Comoros	0	0	0	0	8	n.a.
Congo, Democratic Republic of	4,640	10,389	0	15,029	10	0
Congo, Republic of	1,680	2,881	0	4,561	503	11
Côte d'Ivoire	0	0	0	0	30	n.a.
Ethiopia	1,433	3,275	3,208	7,916	1,585	20
Ghana	941	3,500	3,801	8,242	980	12
Guinea	70	800	0	870	1,002	115
Kenya	0	0	0	0	51	n.a.
Mali	149	895	1,914	2,958	1	0
Mauritania	210	1,100	855	2,165	844	39
Mozambique	2,270	4,300	1,990	8,560	0	0
Niger	244	1,190	1,026	2,460	68	3
Nigeria	10,022	0	0	10,022	5,398	54
Rwanda	82	709	347	1,138	0	0
Senegal	149	164	1,854	2,167	100	5
Sierra Leone	468	994	644	2,106	34	2
Sudan	0	0	0	0	1,330	n.a.
Tanzania	1,613	1,157	2,804	5,574	21	0
Togo	1,423	0	0	1,423	0	2
Zambia	1,403	885	1,875	4,163	0	0
Zimbabwe	0	0	0	0	500	n.a.
Total	28,877	38,621	21,584	89,082	15,764	20

Sources: Paris Club, International Development Association (2007), World Bank–PPIAF Chinese Projects Database (2008).

n.a. = not applicable.

Chinese financing commitments (according to Chinese plus international sources) to the total value of Western debt relief is computed to provide a rough indication of the extent to which the space afforded by debt relief is being used up by contracting new debts to China.

The table confirms that some of the largest beneficiaries of Chinese finance (such as Angola, Sudan, and Zimbabwe) have not been beneficiaries of recent debt relief initiatives. These three countries together received more than one-third of all China's financing commitments. There are only a handful of countries where the value of recent loans contracted to China represents a high share of the value of recent OECD debt relief. Guinea is the only country to have contracted Chinese debt in excess of the value of OECD debt relief. Mauritania has contracted loans equivalent to 40 percent of its OECD debt relief, and Nigeria, loans equivalent to 55 percent.

7.

THE CHANGING LANDSCAPE OF INFRASTRUCTURE FINANCE

The preceding sections analyzed the phenomenon of Chinese finance for African infrastructure projects in Africa in some detail and from a variety of perspectives. To reach a better understanding of the significance and implications of this trend, it is equally important to take a wider-angle view, and place the Chinese contribution in the broader perspective of infrastructure finance in Africa. To do this, it is necessary to compare China both to traditional sources of infrastructure finance, such as official development assistance (ODA) and private participation in infrastructure (PPI), as well as to other non-OECD financiers such as India and the Arab donors. It is important to clarify that all the figures reported in this section are in terms of financing commitments rather than actual disbursements; this is equally true for Chinese finance, traditional ODA, and PPI.

Other Non-OECD Financiers
China is not the only non-OECD player taking a substantial interest in African infrastructure finance. Arab donors have been providing concessional financing for infrastructure projects for some time, and India (primarily through its own Export-Import Bank) has begun to play a significant role in the last couple of years.

Finance from Arab donors is channeled through a number of special funds or development agencies. Of these the most significant ones in terms of the support they provide to African infrastructure projects are the Islamic Development Bank (27 percent), the Arab Bank for Economic Development in Africa (16 percent), the Kuwait Fund for Arab Economic Development

(16 percent), the OPEC Fund (12 percent), and the Saudi Fund (10 percent). Most of the projects are cofinanced with at least one other Arab donor, the most notable example being the 1,250 MW Merowe Dam in Sudan. Four Arab donors, as well as China Ex-Im Bank, jointly committed US$850 million of financing for the construction of the US$1.2 billion dam. Concessional financing is typically provided with interest rates of 1–2 percent and a 20- to 30-year repayment period.

The activities of all these institutions are publicly reported; hence it is straightforward to build up a picture of their project portfolio in Africa. Total commitments by this group of Arab donors were an estimated US$3.6 billion in 2001–07, but there was no discernible year-on-year trend with commitment levels averaging just over US$500 million per year. Project size is relatively small, with an average value of US$22 million. Activities are broadly spread across 36 countries in sub-Saharan Africa, but with evidence of greater concentration in countries with relatively large Muslim populations. Around half of the resources are associated with transportation (mainly roads) projects, a further 30 percent with power, and 15 percent with water and sanitation.

India is also beginning to emerge as a significant new player in African infrastructure finance. A detailed survey of international press reports, similar to that conducted for China, reveals 20 Indian-official or state-owned enterprise (SOE)-funded infrastructure projects worth US$2.6 billion over the period 2003–07, averaging US$0.5 billion per year. Once again no clear trend is apparent, with flows being highly volatile. Similar to the case of China, India's activities in infrastructure finance are closely linked to interests in natural resource development, where a further US$7.3 billion of investments were identified over the same period. As with China, the India Ex-Im Bank is the primary conduit for infrastructure finance, with terms varying according to the nature of the project. For example, in the case of a 2006 Kosti Power Plant in Sudan, India Ex-Im Bank provided a 4 percent interest rate over a nine-year term with four years of grace. As with China, Indian financing has been heavily concentrated in oil-exporting countries, most notably Nigeria and to a lesser extent Sudan.

The bulk of India's financing activity is concentrated in a single Nigerian deal struck in November 2005. At that time, ONGC Mittal (a 50–48 joint venture between state-owned Oil and Natural Gas Corporation [ONGC] and the private Mittal Steel) made a commitment of US$6 billion in Nigeria to build a 9-million-ton-per-year oil refinery, 2,000 MW power plant, and 1,000-kilometer cross-nation railway. It has not been made public how much the refinery and infrastructure will cost, respectively, but it was estimated that (roughly) US$3 billion will go to each.

In Sudan, India has financed some US$600 million of energy infrastructure, including a 741 km oil product pipeline linking the Khartoum refinery to Port Sudan, and four 125 MW Kosti combined cycle power plants and associated transmission system. In parallel, India purchased a 25 percent stake in the Greater Nile Petroleum Operating Company (GNPOC) from the Canadian firm Talisman Energy, including exploration rights for blocks 1, 2, and 4, which are currently producing 280,000 barrels per day. In addition, India has acquired 25 percent stakes in blocks 5A and 5B of the Thar Jath field.

India also became active in Angola's rail sector, committing to a US$40 million project to rehabilitate the Namibe-Matala (Huila) railroad in August of 2004. The project was funded by the India Ex-Im Bank on a concessional basis, with repayment to be made over 50 years. Other than Angola, the Indian consortium Rites and Ircon International (RII) secured a concession contract in December 2004 for the restoration and management of the Beira rail system in central Mozambique. RII promised to invest US$55 million in the system, while the World Bank provided a loan of US$110 million. India's largest rail deal, however, was part of the US$6 billion oil and infrastructure package agreement reached in Nigeria in November 2005, involving the construction of an east-west, 1,000 railway.

Aggregating across these three emerging financiers gives an overall indication of the importance of these new players (figure 19). Through 2003, the combined activities of the emerging financiers amounted to no more than US$0.6–1.4 billion, with the Arab funds being the most important category. Volumes jumped to US$2 billion in 2004 with the emergence of China, topped US$4 billion in 2005 due to major investments by India, peaked at around US$8 billion in 2006 as a result of the Chinese "Year of Africa," and tailed back to around US$5 billion in 2007.

Comparison of OECD and Non-OECD Finance

To put the activities of non-OECD financiers in perspective, it is relevant to compare them to ODA from the OECD countries as well as other conventional sources of infrastructure finance such as PPI (which is essentially a subcategory of FDI). The comparison indicates substantial growth from PPI and non-OECD commitments in recent years. In 2006, the totals provided by PPI and non-OECD financiers were broadly similar, amounting to just over US$8 billion each, followed by ODA total commitments of more than US$5 billion. Both non-OECD and PPI commitments tailed back in 2007, while OECD totals continued to increase (figure 20).

Another important question is the extent to which the emergence of new sources of finance has helped to bridge the infrastructure financing gap in

Figure 19: Non-OECD infrastructure finance in sub-Saharan Africa, 2001–07

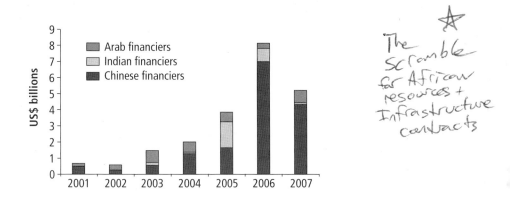

The Scramble for African resources + Infrastructure contracts

Source: World Bank–PPIAF Chinese Projects Database (2008).

Note: Figures for China include only projects that could be confirmed from Chinese sources. Only financing from official or SOE sources is reported.

Figure 20: External infrastructure finance in sub-Saharan Africa, 2001–06

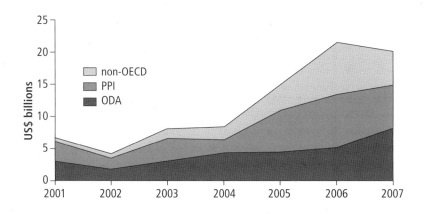

Source: World Bank–PPIAF Chinese Projects Database; World Bank–PPIAF PPI database (ppi.worldbank.org); Infrastructure Consortium for Africa Annual Report, 2008.

Note: Reported PPI data include investments into new and existing projects with financial closure years 2001–07 only.

Figure 21: External infrastructure finance by sector in sub-Saharan Africa, 2001–06

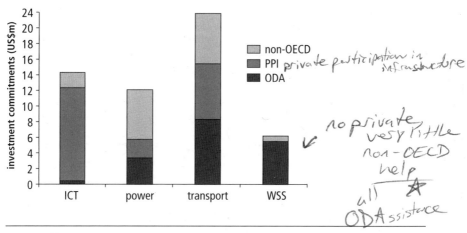

Source: World Bank–PPIAF Chinese Projects Database; World Bank–PPIAF PPI database (ppi.worldbank.org); OECD database (http://stats.oecd.org/).

Note: WSS = Water supply and sanitation.

Africa. Disaggregating by sector, a very different picture emerges in each case (figure 21). In information and communication technology (ICT), the contribution of non-OECD financiers is also relatively small, but comes on top of already abundant resources from the private sector. The contribution of the non-OECD financiers is particularly important in the power sector, where it constitutes a substantial addition to existing flows. In transport, the contribution is relatively more modest, but still significant. In water, the contribution of non-OECD financiers is small in relation to needs. With the exception of ICT, a significant funding gap remains even after taking the contributions of the non-OECD financiers into account.

The foregoing analysis already points to certain sectoral patterns of specialization across the different financiers. Whereas ODA is relatively evenly spread across transport, power, and water, PPI is heavily skewed toward ICT and non-OECD finance is heavily skewed toward the power and transport sectors (figure 22a). The result of this specialization is that the sources of finance vary substantially for each sector (figure 22b). Thus, ICT is almost entirely funded by PPI. Half of the resources for the power sector come from the non-OECD financiers (focused primarily on generation and hydropower), with ODA making the next most substantial contribution (that also encompasses transmission and distribution). About 40 percent of resources for the

Figure 22: Sectoral specialization of external sources of infrastructure finance in sub-Saharan Africa, 2001–06

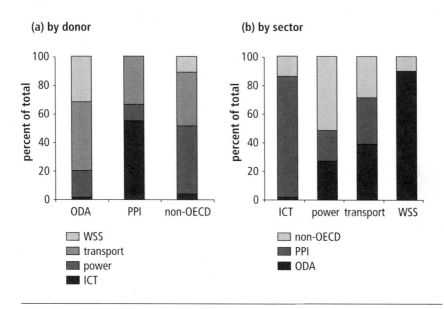

(a) by donor

(b) by sector

Source: World Bank–PPIAF Chinese Projects Database; World Bank–PPIAF PPI database (ppi.worldbank.org); OECD database (http://stats.oecd.org/).

transport sector comes from ODA (focused on roads), with emerging financiers (focused on rail) also making a significant contribution. Finally, the water and sanitation sector is almost exclusively financed by ODA.

To some extent, and without any particular orchestration, the interests of the different financiers appear to be largely complementary. Thus, ODA focuses on social concerns and finance of public goods, PPI seeks the most commercially lucrative opportunities in ICT, and emerging financiers are motivated by the desire to create productive infrastructures.

A similar pattern of specialization emerges with respect to geography, with different countries benefiting disproportionately from different sources of finance. Figure 23 presents the amount of external infrastructure financing flows for the 17 countries that capture more than 2 percent of their GDP in such assistance. Looking across these countries, it is evident that they rely predominantly on different sources of external finance for infrastructure.

The countries that rely predominantly on non-OECD financiers are Guinea, Mauritania, Zimbabwe, Ethiopia, the Central African Republic, and The Gambia. These countries also tend to be among the largest recipients of

Figure 23: Geographic specialization of external sources of infrastructure finance in sub-Saharan Africa

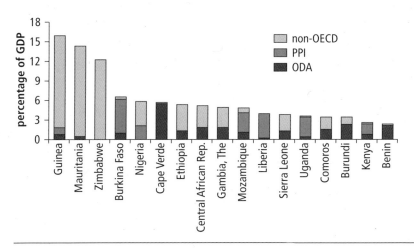

Sources: Three-year average of financing data reported by World Bank–PPIAF Chinese Projects Database, World Bank PPI Database, and OECD International Development Statistics; divided by GDP taken from World Bank World Development Indicators (2008).

external finance. In the case of Guinea, Mauritania, and Zimbabwe, non-OECD finance amounts to more than 10 percent of GDP. The countries most heavily reliant on PPI are Burkina Faso, Liberia, Mozambique, Uganda, and Kenya. The countries most heavily reliant on ODA are Benin, Burundi, and Cape Verde.

8.

CONCLUSION

This study documents the emergence of China as a major new financier of infrastructure in sub-Saharan Africa. Chinese financing commitments rose from around US$0.5 billion per year in the early 2000s to at least US$7 billion in 2006, which was China's official "Year of Africa." Such indirect evidence as exists on the financing terms of these loans suggests that they are more favorable than the private capital markets, though not as soft as ODA. Thus, Chinese loans were found to have an average grant element of 18 percent compared with 54 percent for official creditors.

China is not the only non-OECD financier to be playing a major role in Africa. India is also scaling up finance for infrastructure projects in the region, with commitments averaging $0.5 billion a year over the years 2003–07. Chinese and Indian finance share many common characteristics, including their channeling through the respective countries' Ex-Im banks and their focus on countries that are becoming major petroleum trading partners, such as Nigeria and Sudan. In addition to China and India, the Arab donors are also playing a significant role in African infrastructure finance, with their resources being channeled primarily in the form of soft loans through development funds focusing on roads and other social infrastructure projects.

China's approach to its intergovernmental financial cooperation forms part of a broader phenomenon of south-south economic cooperation between developing nations. The principles underlying this support are therefore ones of mutual benefit, reciprocity, and complementarity. Unlike traditional ODA, financing is not channeled through a development agency, but rather through the Ex-Im Bank with its explicit mission to promote trade. Given the export promotion rationale, the tying of financial support to the participation of contractors from the financing country is a typical feature. A similar approach is currently being taken by the India Ex-Im Bank, and has in the past been used by export credit agencies of other countries.

Even compared to other developing regions, sub-Saharan Africa faces a serious infrastructure deficit that is currently undermining growth and competitiveness. The estimated infrastructure financing needs are on the order of US$22 billion per year, with an associated funding gap of over US$10 billion per year. Against this context, the growth of Chinese (and other emerging) finance presents itself as an encouraging trend for the region, and can potentially make a material contribution to closing the deficit. In the power sector, for example, the 10 hydropower plants currently agreed upon or under construction amount to at least 6,000 MW of capacity and when completed would represent a 30 percent increase over and above existing hydrocapacity in the region.

To put these findings in perspective, the combined contribution of China and the other emerging financiers at more than US$8 billion for 2006 is broadly comparable to private participation in infrastructure (PPI) and exceeds the combined official development assistance of the OECD countries that topped US$5 billion in the same year. The analysis shows a significant degree of complementarity in the sectoral and geographic focus of traditional and emerging finance. Non-OECD donors tend to focus on productive infrastructures, mainly power (in particular hydroelectric schemes) and railways, and direct their resources primarily to major petroleum trading partners. Traditional donors tend to focus on public goods such as roads, water, sanitation, and electrification and spread their support more evenly, reaching non-resource-exporting countries to a greater extent.

The advent of China and other non-OECD players as major financiers presents itself as a hopeful trend for Africa, given the magnitude of its infrastructure deficit. The aid provided by these emerging financiers is unprecedented in scale and in its focus on large-scale infrastructure projects. With new actors and new modalities, there is a learning process ahead for borrowers and financiers alike. The key challenge for African governments will be how to make the best strategic use of all external sources of infrastructure funding, including those of emerging financiers.

BIBLIOGRAPHY

Akyut, Dilek, and Andrea Goldstein. Forthcoming. "Foreign Direct Investment in the Oil Sector." Mimeo, OECD Development Centre, Paris.

———. 2006. "Developing Country Multinationals: South-South Investment Comes of Age." Working Paper No. 257, OECD Development Centre, Paris.

Alden, C., and A. Rothman. 2006. *China and Africa Special Report: Terms of Endearment from Marxism to Material.* Shanghai: CLSA Asia-Pacific Markets.

Bosshard, P. 2007. China's Role in Financing African Infrastructure. International Rivers Network.

Bosshard, P. 2008. China's Environmental Footprint in Africa. Pambazuka News 282, http://www.pambazuka.org/en/category/comment/48442.

Brautigam, D. 1997. Chinese Aid and African Development: Exporting Green Revolution. Basingstoke: Palgrave Macmillan.

Broadman, Harry. 2006. *Africa's Silk Road: China and India's New Economic Frontier.* Washington, DC: World Bank.

Burnside, C., and D. Dollar. 2000. "Aid, Policies, and Growth." *American Economic Review* 90(4): 847–68.

———. 2004. "Aid, Policies, and Growth: Revisiting the Evidence." Policy Research Working Paper No. 3251, World Bank, Washington, DC.

Calderon, Cesar, and Luis Serven. 2004. "The Effects of Infrastructure Development on Growth and Income Distribution." Policy Research Working Paper No. WPS 3400, World Bank, Washington, DC.

Campos, I., and A. Vines. 2008. "Angola and China A Pragmatic Partnership." Working Paper, Washington, DC: Center for Strategic and International Studies (CSIS).

Chaponnière, J. R. 2007. "La Chine: une aide difficile à mesurer" La Lettre des Economistes de l'AFD No. 15, Agence Française de Développement, Paris.

Chen, C., P. Chiu, R. Orr, and A. Goldstein. 2007. *An Empirical Analysis of Chinese Construction Firms' Entry into Africa.* Conference paper, CRIOCM2007, "International Symposium on Advancement of Construction Management and Real Estate," Sydney, Australia.

Corkin, L. 2006. *China's Interest and Activity in Angola's Construction and Infrastructure Sectors.* Centre for Chinese Studies, University of Stellenbosch.

Corkin, L. 2007. "The Strategic Entry of China's Emerging Multinationals into Africa." *China Report* 2007 43: 309.

Davies, M., H. Edinger, N. Tay, and S. Naidu. 2008. *How China Delivers Development Assistance to Africa.* Centre for Chinese Studies, University of Stellenbosch.

Downs, E. 2007. "The Fact and Fiction of Sino-African Energy Relation." *China Security* 3(3): 42–68.

Esfahani, H. S., and M. T. Ramirez. 2003. "Institutions, Infrastructure, and Economic Growth." *Journal of Development Economics* 70: 443–77.

Estache, A. 2005. "What Do We Know about Sub-Saharan Africa's Infrastructure and the Impact of the 1990s Reforms?" Mimeo, World Bank, Washington, DC.

Evans, P. C., and E. S. Downs. 2006. "Untangling China's Quest for Oil through State-Backed Financial Deals." Brief No. 154, Brookings Institution, Washington, DC.

Gill, B., C. Huang, and J. S. Morrison. 2007. *China's Expanding Role in Africa: Implications for the United States.* Washington, DC: Center for Strategic and International Studies.

Glosny, M. A. 2006. *China's Foreign Aid Policy: Lifting States out of Poverty or Leaving Them to the Dictators?* CSIS Freeman Report, Center for Strategic and International Studies, Washington, DC.

Goldstein, A., N. Pinaud, H. Reisen, and X. Chen. 2006. *The Rise of China and India: What's In It for Africa?* Organisation for Economic Co-operation and Development, Paris.

HRW. 2001. *Human Rights Watch World Report 2000.* Human Rights Watch (www.hrw.org).

IMF (International Monetary Fund) and World Bank. 2006. *Applying the Debt Sustainability Framework for Low-Income Countries Post-Debt Relief.*

IMF. 2006. "IDA Countries and Non-Concessional Debt: Dealing with the 'Free Rider' in IDA14 Grant-Recipient and Post-MDRI Countries." Resource Mobilization Department.

IMF. 2006. *Direction of Trade Statistics Yearbook 2006.*

Infrastructure Consortium for Africa. 2007. *ICA Annual Report 2006.* Infrastructure Consortium for Africa Secretariat, Tunis.

Jacquet, P., J. R. Chaponnière, O. Delefosse, and V. Jacquelain. 2007. "La Chine, Moteur du Développement." La Lettre des Economistes de l'AFD No. 15, Agence Française de Développement, Paris.

Johnston, D. 1994. International *Petroleum Fiscal Systems and Production-Sharing Contracts.* Pennwel.

King, Kenneth. 2006. "China's Partnership Discourse with Africa." NEPAD conference paper. *China in Africa in the 21st Century: Preparing for the Forum on China-Africa Cooperation* organied by the Royal African Society, the South African Institute of International Affairs, and the Secretariat of NEPAD (the New Partnership for Africa's Development), 16-17 October 2006, Muldersdrift, near Johannesburg.

Kurlantzick, Joshua. 2006. "Beijing's Safari: China's Move into Africa and Its Implications for Aid, Development, and Governance." Carnegie Endowment for International Peace Policy Outlook.

Ministry of Foreign Affairs. 2006. "China's African Policy." Web site of the Ministry of Foreign Affairs of China: http://www.fmprc.gov.cn/eng/zxxx/t230615.htm.

Moss, Todd, and Sarah Rose. 2006. "China Ex-Im Bank and Africa: New Lending, New Challenges." Center for Global Development Notes (November).

Muneku, A., and G. Koyi. 2007. *The Social Impact of Asian FDI in Zambia. A Case of Chinese and Indian Investments in the Extractive Industry in Zambia (1997–2007).*

Mwase, N. 1983. "The Tanzania-Zambia Railway: The Chinese Loan and the Pre-Investment Analysis Revisited." *The Journal of Modern African Studies* 21 (3): 535–43.

Ndulu, B. 2004. *Infrastructure, Regional Integration, and Growth in Sub-Saharan Africa: Dealing with the Disadvantage of Geography and Sovereign Fragmentation.* Background paper for the Commission for Africa.

Nellis, J. 2006. *Back to the Future for African Infrastructure: Why State Ownership Is No More Promising the Second Time Around?* Working Paper No. 84, Center for Global Development, Washington, DC.

Nielson, D. L., and M. J. Tierney. 2003. "Delegation to International Organizations: Agency Theory and World Bank Environmental Reform." *International Organization* 57: 241–76.

Pambazuka. 2006. *African Perspectives on China in Africa.* Pambazuka News 282, Ghana.

Shelton, C. 2005. *China and Africa: Understanding the Growing Trade and Investment Relationship.* The Corporate Council on Africa.

University of Stellenbosch Centre for Chinese Studies. 2006. *China's Interest and Activity in Africa's Construction and Infrastructure Sector.* Stellenbosch University, South Africa.

Yepes, T., J. Pierce, and V. Foster. 2007. *Making Sense of Sub-Saharan Africa's Infrastructure Endowment: A Benchmarking Approach.* Mimeo, Sustainable Development Department, Africa Region, World Bank, Washington, DC.

Zhang, Z. X. 2006. *China's Hunt for Oil in Perspective.* East-West Center, Honolulu.

ANNEX 1.

METHODOLOGY FOR SEARCHING FACTIVA DATABASE

Factiva is a news database that covers 10,000 different media from 159 countries. Using the Factiva search engine it is possible to do very precise targeted searches for news coverage of specific topics. This annex documents the search terms that were used to generate the database of Chinese infrastructure and natural resource projects in Africa.

Factiva uses simple, logical statements as search parameters. For example, to find articles containing two specific words used in the same article, such as "China" and "Africa," the operator "and" is used. To find articles using either of two words, such as "China" or "Africa," the operator "or" is used. The * parameter controls for different endings of words. For example, Chin* would pick up the use of "China" or "Chinese" or "China's" in an article. The parameter w/7, for example, finds two words within 7 words of each other, for example, China w/7 Africa, would find articles with the word "China" within 7 words of "Africa."

The construction of the project database began with a broad, general search that was then followed up by specific searches for each country in Africa. The same approach was adapted to obtain information on infrastructure and natural resource projects, as well as debt relief, for both China and India.

Broad, General Search

A number of combinations of search terms was used to do the first-order searches. The initial searches took the following forms:

((china or Chinese) w/10 Africa*) and (invest* or loan or grant or finance or Ex-Im or ex-im or export-import or aid) and (infrastructure or energy or electricity or water or wastewater or sewage or road* or rail* or *port or telecom* or mobile)

((china or Chinese) w/10 Africa*) and (chin* w/5 Ex-Im or ex-im or export-import)

These types of searches generated a very large number of results. To analyze the results, it was necessary to control for either dates or specific countries using "Select Sources: Factiva Intelligent Indexing" located below the search field.

The search terms are bolded in the text of the articles that are identified by the Factiva database. All the articles were initially scanned to identify which were the most informative on project details.

Once a specific project was identified, a follow-up search was conducted using the name of the project or project sponsors to get additional information. For example, if the search revealed an article containing information on the Merowe dam, and reported financing by the China Ex-Im Bank, the follow-up search would be as follows:

(China or Chinese) and Merowe and Sudan and (Ex-Im or ex-im or export-import)

Specific Country Searches

Thereafter, the search process was narrowed to specific countries. Two different approaches were used to do this.

The first approach, which proved to yield quite efficient results, was the following:

((China or Chinese) w/10 (Angola or Benin or Botswana or Burkina or Burundi)) and (infrastructure or energy or electricity or water or wastewater or sewage or road* or rail* or *port or telecom* or mobile) and (invest* or loan or grant or finance or Ex-Im or ex-im or export-import or aid)

Alternatively, Factiva also allows the user to specifically control for country by clicking "region" under "Select Sources: Factiva Intelligent Indexing" then selecting "Developing Economies" selecting a specific country and then just running a basic search such as the following.

(China or Chinese) and (infrastructure or energy or electricity or water or wastewater or sewage or road* or rail* or *port or telecom* or mobile) and (invest* or loan or grant or finance or Ex-Im or ex-im or export-import or aid)

To find information on China's debt relief activities, the following terms were used:

((china or Chinese) w/10 (Rwanda or São Tomé or Senegal or Seychelles or Sierra Leone or Somalia or Sudan or Swaziland or Tanzania or Togo or Uganda or Zambia or Zimbabwe)) and ((debt*) w/7 (relief or forgive or cancel* or reduc* or waive or writ* off))

To find information about natural resource development projects supported by China or India, the following terms were used:

((China or Chinese) w/10 (insert countries here)) and (CNOCC or Sinopec or CNPC or PetroChina or mineral*)

((India* w/10 (insert countries here)) and (ONGC or OVL or GAIL or Oil India or Indian Oil or mineral*)

Similar searches were also conducted inserting names of specific minerals such as copper, bauxite, ore, manganese, coal, and so forth.

ANNEX 2.

METHODOLOGY FOR CREATING PROJECT DATABASE

To systematically record the information that was found in the newspaper articles generated by the Factiva database, a database structure was predesigned. The articles generated by Factiva were then read with a view to filling the specific data fields described below, which were entered into the database to create consistent project records. Only 2001–07 projects were targeted.

Infrastructure Projects
The database records Chinese-financed projects in sub-Saharan Africa that involve the infrastructure sectors (power, transport, ICT, water, and sanitation). It also allows the collection of similar information for projects financed by Indian and Arab financiers. The key pieces of information collected are described below:

- **Agreement date.** Recorded when an official announcement in the press is made concerning a government or Arab donor-funded commitment or when a Chinese or Indian company formally agrees to undertake a project. In the case where the exact date is uncertain, the earliest recorded date of when the project financing was announced is used. It must be clear that a formal commitment has been made (for example, formal documents were signed) to qualify as a project.
- **Status.** The main categories are: agreed, under construction, and completed, or under reconsideration.

- **Sector** (for example, transport); subsector, for example, road, railway, airport). Sometimes, commitments of funds will be for "general infrastructure purposes" or involve commitments for more than one sector. In those cases where it is unclear how a given commitment will be divided up among specific infrastructure sectors and subsectors, the sector is recorded as "General." The database does not count commitments given for unspecified purposes or for "projects to be determined at a later date," because it is unclear in those cases that the resources will be directed toward traditional infrastructure.
- **Chinese financier.** Most of the projects were funded by the China Ex-Im Bank, the Indian Ex-Im Bank, Arab donors, or state-owned enterprises. Sometimes, it is unclear which specific institution is committing resources as reports in the press refer simply to, for example, "the Chinese government" as the source of the funds. Such cases are recorded as "Chinese government—Unspecified" in the database.
- **Type of financing.** The database records a commitment as a loan, concessional loan, grant, or equity financed. The type of financing is recorded as it is most commonly referred to in public media. That is, there is no objective interest rate below which the database records loans as "concessional." Oftentimes, the terms of financing are confidential; in those cases the project is simply recorded as a "loan." For the Arab donors, it seemed clear that most of the project financing should be deemed "concessional" because interest rates were generally 1–2 percent, over 20–30 years. If detailed financing terms are available, they are recorded as well.
- **Amount of financing.** Only that portion of the total project cost that is attributable to Chinese funding sources is recorded, not the total value of the contract. For example, if a hydroelectric dam cost US$700 million, and the China Ex-Im Bank financed US$500 of that while the government of the country in question financed the remainder, only the US$500 is recorded as the Chinese commitment, while the US$700 million would be recorded as the total project cost. Likewise, in the case of a sponsor-financed project, only the amount(s) attributable to the sponsor(s) are recorded. In a project in which a sponsor has a share of the equity, and only the total value of the project is known, the equity stake is multiplied by the total project value to get the sponsor commitment.
- **Contractor.** Sometimes the specific names of these firms are not made public, yet it is clear that the project agreement requires, for example, Chinese-owned entities to be contracted for the work. Such cases are recorded as "Chinese contractors—Unspecified." For the projects financed by Arab

donors, there was little information available on the winners of the construction contracts.

- Whether or not there was a **natural resource or political consideration** involved in the project—either directly or indirectly. Most Chinese government-funded projects in sub-Saharan Africa are ultimately aimed at securing a flow of sub-Saharan Africa's natural resources for export to China. Oftentimes, commitments of funds to infrastructure projects either precede or follow an agreement for a Chinese firm to exploit oil, mineral, or other natural resources in the project country. Other times, Chinese loans for projects will be backed by guarantees of natural resource exports. The database attempts to record this trend by linking projects to natural resource deals when such links are readily apparent or deemed appropriate. Other times, it is determined that projects are for purely commercial reasons and recorded as such. Again, however, there is no rigorous methodology used in this classification.
- **Other project details.** A brief "project description" is included in every entry that attempts to capture the capacity (size) of the project, location, duration, and other details deemed interesting.

Natural Resource Project Database

The natural resource database records projects with Chinese, Indian, or Arab involvement in sub-Saharan Africa's natural resource sector (that is, oil and minerals) and subsector (oil exploration, oil refining, chrome, copper, and so forth) and captures the same project information as the infrastructure database. It is important to note that commitments to the natural resource projects are considered FDI.

SUMMARY OF CHINESE-FUNDED INFRASTRUCTURE PROJECTS BY SECTOR

Table A3.1: Overview of Chinese financing commitments in confirmed power projects in sub-Saharan Africa, 2001–07

Country	Year	Status	Project	Chinese financier	Contractors	Added capacity	Project cost (US$m)	Chinese commitments (US$m)
HYDRO GENERATION								
Benin	2004	Construction	Adjarala Dam on the Mono River, Benin's share	Ex-Im Bank, China	Unknown	96 MW	162	Unconfirmed
Burundi	2005	Construction	Rehabilitation of Gikonge and Ruvyironza hydraulic power plants	Government, China	Xing Jiang Bei Xin Construction Engineering (group) Co., Ltd	2.5 MW	—	—
Congo, Rep. of	2001	Construction	Construction of Congo River Dam at Imboulou	Ex-Im Bank, China	China National Machinery & Equipment Import & Export Corp. (CMEC); Sinohydro	120 MW	280	280
Ethiopia	2002	Construction	Construction of the Tekeze Dam, in the state of Tigray in Ethiopia	Ex-Im Bank, China	China National Water Resources and Hydro-power Engineering Corp. (CWHEC)	300 MW	224	50
Gabon	2006	Agreement	Poubara hydropower dam (part of US$ 3 billion Belinga iron ore project)	Ex-Im Bank, China	Sinohydro	—	—	—

Country	Year	Status	Project	Chinese financier	Contractors	Added capacity	Project cost (US$m)	Chinese commitments (US$m)
Ghana	2007	Construction	Bui Dam Complex	Ex-Im Bank, China	Sinohydro	400 MW	622	562
Guinea	2004	Completed	Rehabilitation of Ginkang hydropower plant and Tinkisso Hydropower plant	Government, China	Hunan Construction Engineering Group Corp.	—	2	2
Guinea	2006	Under reconsideration	Souapiti Dam project on the Konkouri River	Ex-Im Bank, China	Sinohydro	750 MW	1,000	1,000
Mozambique	2006	Under reconsideration	Mphanda Nkuwa Dam, and transmission line to Maputo	To be defined	Camargo Correa	1,300 MW	2,300	—
Nigeria	2006	Under reconsideration	Construction of Mambilla hydroelectric power plant in Taraba State	Ex-Im Bank, China	China Gezhouba Group Corporation (CGGC); China Geo-Engineering Corporation (CGC)	2,600 MW	1,460	1,000
Sudan	2003	Construction	Construction of the Merowe hydroelectric dam	Ex-Im Bank, China	Sinohydro	1,250 MW	1,200	400

(continued)

Table A3.1: continued

Country	Year	Status	Project	Chinese financier	Contractors	Added capacity	Project cost (US$m)	Chinese commitments (US$m)
Togo	2004	Construction	Adjarala Dam on the Mono River, Togo's share	Ex-Im Bank, China	Sinohydro	96 MW	162	Unconfirmed
Uganda	2006	Unknown	Construction of the Ayago-Nile Dam	Unconfirmed	Unknown	530 MW	900	Unconfirmed
Zambia	2005	Agreement	Kafue Gorge lower power station project	Ex-Im Bank, China	Sinohydro	750 MW	600	—
Zambia	2007	Construction	Expansion of Kariba North Bank hydraulic power plant on Zambezi river	Ex-Im Bank, China	Sinohydro	360 MW	280	Unconfirmed
Hydro generation total								3,294
THERMAL GENERATION								
Ghana	2007	Agreement	Construction of gas-stream combined-cycle power generation plant at Krone, near Tema	CADF; Shenzhen	Shenzhen Energy Investment Co., Ltd; China Africa Development Fund (CADF)	200 MW	143	137

Country	Year	Status	Project	Chinese financier	Contractors	Added capacity	Project cost (US$m)	Chinese commitments (US$m)
Nigeria	2005	Construction	Construction of Papalanto power gas turbine power plant, in Ogun	Ex-Im Bank, China	Sepco	335 MW	360	298
Nigeria	2005	Construction	Construction of Okitipupa (Omotosho) gas turbine power plant, in Ondo	Ex-Im Bank, China	CMEC	335 MW	361	—
Nigeria	2005	Construction	Construction of Geregu gas turbine power plant	Ex-Im Bank, China	Siemens	138 MW	390	—
Senegal	2006	Agreement	Construction of a power plant equipped with two turbines	Government, China	China Metallurgical Group	250 MW	—	—
Sudan	2001	Completed	Construction of the El-Gaili combined-cycle power plant, Phase 1	Ex-Im Bank, China	Harbin Power Equipment Company Limited (HPEC)	200 MW	150	128
Sudan	2005	Agreement	500 MW coal-fired power plant in Port Sudan; 320 MW gas-fired power plant in Rabak	Ex-Im Bank, China	Shandong Electric Power Constr. Corp. (SEPCO)	820 MW	—	512

(continued)

Table A3.1: *continued*

Country	Year	Status	Project	Chinese financier	Contractors	Added capacity	Project cost (US$m)	Chinese commitments (US$m)
Sudan	2007	Completed	Construction of the El-Gaili (Al Jaily) power plant, Phase 2	Ex-Im Bank, China	HPEC	100 MW	—	—
Sudan	2007	Construction	Construction of 300 MW gas-fired power plant in Al-Fulah	Ex-Im Bank, China	Shandong Electric Power Constr. Corp. (SEPCO)	300 MW	518	—
Togo	2007	Completed	Equip the township of Tomegbe with a high-capacity generating unit	Government, China	Unknown	—	—	—
Zimbabwe	2004	Agreement	Construction of two electricity generation units at Hwange Power Station	CATIC	China National Aero-Technology Import & Export Co. (CATIC)	—	500	500
Zimbabwe	2006	Under reconsideration	Construction of coal mines and three thermal power stations in Dande	Government, China	CMEC	600 MW	1,300	—
Thermal generation total								1,574

DISTRIBUTION, TRANSMISSION, AND GENERAL

Country	Year	Status	Project	Chinese financier	Contractors	Added capacity	Project cost (US$m)	Chinese commitments (US$m)
Angola	2002	Completed	Rehabilitation and extension of the power system in Luanda, Phase 1	Ex-Im Bank, China	China Machine-Building International Corporation (CMIC)	—	15	15
Angola	2004	Completed	Rehabilitation and extension of the Lubango power transmission project	Unconfirmed	China National Electronics Import and Export Corp. (CEIEC)	—	15	Unconfirmed
Angola	2004	Completed	Power portion of the first phase of 2004 US$ 2 billion loan from Ex-Im Bank of China	Ex-Im Bank, China	Multiple	—	—	200
Angola	2005	Completed	Rehabilitation and extension of the power system in Luanda, Phase 2	Ex-Im Bank, China		—	46	46

(continued)

Table A3.1: *continued*

Country	Year	Status	Project	Chinese financier	Contractors	Added capacity	Project cost (US$m)	Chinese commitments (US$m)
Angola	2006	Completed	Capanda-Ndalatando and Cambambe-Luanda transmission lines	Ex-Im Bank, China	China Railway Construction Corporation (CRCC)	—	—	—
Ghana	2006	Construction	The electrification of rural areas in Ghana	Ex-Im Bank, China	China International Water & Electric Corp. (CWE)	—	90	81
Senegal	2007	Construction	Construction of power transmission line and 4 transformer substations	Ex-Im Bank, China	CMEC	30 km	70	49
Sudan	2003	Construction	Power transmission and transformation line for the Merowe hydroelectric dam	Ex-Im Bank, China	HPEC; Jilin Province Transmission and Substation Company	1,776 km	—	—
Sudan	2006	Construction	National Electricity Corporation (NEC) transition line	Ex-Im Bank, China	CMEC	340 km	81	81
Distribution, transmission and general total								*472*
POWER TOTAL								**5,340**

Source: World Bank–PPIAF Chinese Projects Database (2008).

Table A3.2: Overview of Chinese financing commitments in confirmed transport projects in sub-Saharan Africa, 2001–07

Country	Year	Status	Project	Chinese financier	Contractors	Added capacity (US$ m)	Project cost (US$ m)	Chinese commitments (US$ m)
AIRPORT								
Comoros	2004	Completed	Rehabilitation of Prince Said Ibrahim International Airport in Moroni	Ex-Im Bank, China	China Airport Construction Group Corporation of Civil Aviation Administration of China (CAAC)	—	—	8
Congo, Rep. of	2007	Construction	Construction of terminals, tower, and power control center at Ollombo Airport	Ex-Im Bank, China	China Jiangsu International Economic-Technical Cooperation Corporation	—	56	56
Congo, Rep. of	2007	Construction	Rehabilitate Brazaville Airport project (Maya-Maya International Airport)	Ex-Im Bank, China	Weihai International Economic & Technical Cooperative Co., Ltd. (WIETC)	—	160	160
Mauritania	2005	Construction	Construction of a new international airport at Nouakchott	Government, China	Unknown	—	280	224
Airport total								448

(continued)

Table A3.2: *continued*

Country	Year	Status	Project	Chinese financier	Contractors	Added capacity	Project cost (US$ m)	Chinese commitments (US$ m)
BRIDGE								
Ethiopia	2006	Construction	Construction of the Gotera Intersection bridge in Addis Ababa	Ex-Im Bank, China	Shanghai Construction Group	—	13	13
Mali	2007	Agreement	Grant to construct the third bridge for Mali in Bamako	Ministry of Commerce, China	Unknown	—	—	—
Niger	2007	Construction	Construction of the bridge over River Niger in Niamey	Ministry of Commerce, China	No.14 China Railway Group Co., Ltd.	2.15	40	40
Sudan	2004	Construction	Construction of the bridge between Khartoum and the Sudanese-Egyptian border	China National Petroleum Corporation (CNPC)	Jilin Province International Economy & Trade Development Corporation (JIETDC)	0.44	20	10

Country	Year	Status	Project	Chinese financier	Contractors	Added capacity	Project cost (US$ m)	Chinese commitments (US$ m)
Sudan	2006	Construction	Construction of Ruffa bridge	China Poly Group Corporation	China Poly Group Corporation; China Railway 18th Bureau Group Co. Ltd.	0.394	23	—
Bridge total								62
RAILWAY								
Angola	2003	Completed	Rehabilitation of Luanda railway, Phase 1	Government, China	CMEC	43	90	90
Botswana	2006	Proposed	Construct the Trans-Kgalagadi railway that would link Botswana with Namibia	Ex-Im Bank, China	Unknown	—	—	—
Gabon	2006	Agreement	Belinga-Santa Clara railway (part of US$3 billion Belinga iron ore project)	Ex-Im Bank, China	China Railway Engineering Group Co. Ltd. (CREGC)	—	—	—

(continued)

Table A3.2: continued

Country	Year	Status	Project	Chinese financier	Contractors	Added capacity	Project cost (US$ m)	Chinese commitments (US$ m)
Mauritania	2007	Agreement	Build 430 km railway from Nouakchott to Bofal	Ex-Im Bank, China	Transtech Engineering Corporation	430	620	620
Namibia	2005	Completed	Railway equipment purchase	Ex-Im Bank, China	China Railway Material Group	—	200	31
Nigeria	2006	Under reconsideration	Modernization of the Nigeria railway, Phase 1: Lagos-Kano railway	Ex-Im Bank, China	China Civil Engineering Construction Corporation (CCECC)	1,315	8,300	2,500
Nigeria	2006	Under reconsideration	Abuja Rail Mass Transit Project	Ex-Im Bank, China	China Guangdong Xinguang International Group	—	2,000	1,000
Sudan	2004	Completed	Interest-free loan for railway development	Unconfirmed	China National Petroleum Corporation (CNPC)	—	—	Unconfirmed
Sudan	2007	Agreement	Construction of railway from Khartoum to Port Sudan	Unconfirmed	CREGC	762	1,154	—
Railway total								4,241

ROAD

Country	Year	Status	Project	Chinese financier	Contractors	Added capacity	Project cost (US$ m)	Chinese commitments (US$ m)
Angola	2004	Construction	The no. 1 and 2 ring roads of Angola City	Ex-Im Bank, China	CMEC	51.25	170	170
Angola	2005	Construction	Rehabilitation of the Kifangondo-Caxito-Uige-Negage road	Ex-Im Bank, China	China Road and Bridge Corporation (CRBC)	371	211	211
Botswana	2003	Completed	Letlhakeng-Kang road, Phase 1	Ex-Im Bank, China	CSCEC	561	29	23
Botswana	2006	Construction	Letlhakeng-Kang road, Phase 2	Ex-Im Bank, China	CSCEC	85	40	19
Botswana	2006	Construction	Dutlwe-Morwamosu Road	Ex-Im Bank, China	CSCEC	—	—	17
Chad	2007	Construction	Rehabilitate 6 roads in N'Djamena	Ministry of Commerce, China	Guangdong Provincial Construction Engineering Group Co.	9.7	—	—
Congo, Rep. of	2007	Construction	Road linking Brazaville and Pointe-Noire	Ex-Im Bank, China	CSCEC	178	—	—

(continued)

Table A3.2: *continued*

Country	Year	Status	Project	Chinese financier	Contractors	Added capacity (US$ m)	Project cost (US$ m)	Chinese commitments (US$ m)
Equatorial Guinea	2001	Completed	Niefang-Nkue Road	Government, China	CRBC	33.2	11	11
Equatorial Guinea	2003	Completed	Bata-Niefang section road rehabilitation	Government, China	China Wuyi Co., Ltd.	30	—	6
Ethiopia	2003	Completed	Gottera-Wolo Sefer Road	Government, China	CRBC	2.6	5	3
Ethiopia	2004	Completed	Addis Ababa city ring road, Phase 2	Government, China	CRBC	33.4	77	13
Ethiopia	2006	Agreement	Road and two bridges construction in Addis Ababa	Government, China	CRBC	5.8	17	6
Gabon	2007	Construction	Grant to rehabilitate 17 roads in Gabon	Ministry of Commerce, China	China Geo-Engineering Corporation (CGC)	9.96	—	—
Ghana	2003	Completed	Accra-Kumasi trunk road rehabilitation	Ex-Im Bank, China	CREGC	17.4	23	23

Country	Year	Status	Project	Chinese financier	Contractors	Added capacity (US$ m)	Project cost (US$ m)	Chinese commitments (US$ m)
Kenya	2006	Construction	Rehabilitation of the roads in Nairobi from Kenyatta International Airport to UN Environment Programme	Government, China	CRBC	26	—	28
Kenya	2007	Construction	Grant to construct roads in Nairobi	Ministry of Commerce, China	Shengli Engineering Construction (Group) Corporation Ltd.	22.5	23	23
Mada-gascar	2003	Completed	Rehabilitation of roads in the north of the capital	Ex-Im Bank, China	Anhui Foreign Economic & Trade Development Co.	—	—	—
Rwanda	2003	Completed	Construction of a 2.6 km road in Kigali City	Ex-Im Bank, China	CRBC	—	—	—
Road total								553
TRANSPORT TOTAL								**5,304**

Source: World Bank–PPIAF Chinese Projects Database (2008).

Table A3.3: Overview of Chinese financing commitments in confirmed ICT projects in sub-Saharan Africa, 2001–07

Country	Year	Status	Project	Chinese financier	Contractors	Added capacity (US$ m)	Project cost (US$ m)	Chinese commitments (US$ m)
Angola	2002	Completed	Angola Telecom Network Expansion Project in the Province of Namibe, Huile, Cunene, and Lunda Norte, Phase 1	Ex-Im Bank, China	Alcatel Shanghai Bell (ASB)	—	60	—
Angola	2004	Completed	Telecom portion of the second phase of 2004 US$2 billion loan from Ex-Im Bank of China	Ex-Im Bank, China	Unknown	—	—	200
Angola	2005	Completed	An agreement between ZTE and Mundo Startel to install a new fixed-line network in 8 states across Angola	Ex-Im Bank, China	Zhong Xing Telecommunication Equipment Company Limited (ZTE)	—	69	38
Benin	2004	Completed	Provision of complete GSM national network in Benin—including General Packet Radio Services (GPRS) capability on its existing GSM network	Unknown	ZTE	156	—	—

Country	Year	Status	Project	Chinese financier	Contractors	Added capacity	Project cost (US$ m)	Chinese commitments (US$ m)
Burundi	2004	Completed	Burundi GSM mobile telecommunication project	Ex-Im Bank, China	Huawei Technologies Co., Ltd.	60	9	8
Central African Republic	2005	Completed	Supply and installation for mobile and fixed networks covering the whole country	Ex-Im Bank, China	ZTE	300	79	67
Congo, Dem. Rep. of	2001	Completed	China-Congo Telecom (CCT) network project	Ex-Im Bank, China	ZTE	—	20	10
Côte d'Ivoire	2006	Agreement	Build the network covering Abidjan and its adjacent areas, Phase 1	Ex-Im Bank, China	ZTE	—	30	30
Eritrea	2005	Construction	200,000 fixed-line telecom network rehabilitation project	Ex-Im Bank, China	ZTE	200	21	—
Ethiopia	2003	Completed	Expansion of Ethiopia's existing mobile network capacity in Addis Ababa and regions	Unknown	ZTE	250	29	—

(continued)

Table A3.3: *continued*

Country	Year	Status	Project	Chinese financier	Contractors	Added capacity (US$ m)	Project cost (US$ m)	Chinese commitments (US$ m)
Ethiopia	2006	Agreement	Expand and upgrade Ethiopia's telecom network[a]	Ex-Im Bank, China	ZTE	8,500	—	822
Ethiopia	2007	Construction	First phase of fiber transmission backbone, expansion of mobile phone service for the Ethiopian millennium, and expansion of wireless telephone service[a]	Ex-Im Bank, China	ZTE	—	200	200
Ethiopia	2007	Construction	GSM project phase II[a]	Ex-Im Bank, China	ZTE	—	478	478
Gambia, The	2005	Completed	CDMA network for Gamtel	Unknown	Huawei	—	—	—
Ghana	2003	Completed	Ghana Telecom equipment supply, Phase 1	Ex-Im Bank, China	ASB	—	200	79
Ghana	2005	Agreement	Ghana Telecom equipment supply, Phase 2	Government, China; Sinosure	ASB	—	80	67

Country	Year	Status	Project	Chinese financier	Contractors	Added capacity (US$ m)	Project cost (US$ m)	Chinese commitments (US$ m)
Ghana	2005	Completed	Build a CDMA2000 1X network for Kasapa Telecom	Unknown	ZTE	500	—	—
Ghana	2006	Construction	National Fibre Backbone Project	Ex-Im Bank, China	Huawei	—	70	31
Ghana	2007	Construction	Communication system for security agencies project	Ex-Im Bank, China	ZTE	—	—	Unconfirmed
Lesotho	2007	Agreement	Rehabilitate the Telecom Agricultural Network	Ex-Im Bank, China	ZTE	—	—	30
Lesotho	2007	Construction	Grant to establish television systems in several cities	Ministry of Commerce, China	Unknown	—	—	3
Mali	2005	Agreement	Rehabilitate CDMA2000 1X WLL network in Bamako	ZTE	ZTE	—	2	1
Mauritius	2006	Construction	Milcom purchase by China Mobile	Unknown	China Mobile	250	—	—

(continued)

Table A3.3: *continued*

Country	Year	Status	Project	Chinese financier	Contractors	Added capacity	Project cost (US$ m)	Chinese commitments (US$ m)
Niger	2001	Completed	Niger Telecommunications Company (SONITEL) with GSM mobile system covering the city of Niamey	Unknown	ZTE	—	8	Unconfirmed
Niger	2001	Completed	Tender for 51 percent ownership of SONITEL, Niger's state telecoms company, and its mobile arm, Sahel Com	ZTE	ZTE	—	—	24
Nigeria	2002	Construction	National Rural Telephony Project (NRPT), Phase 1	Ex-Im Bank, China	Huawei; ZTE; ASB	150	200	200
Nigeria	2006	Completed	Nigeria First Communication Sattelite NigComSat-1	Ex-Im Bank, China	China Great Wall Industry Corporation	—	—	200
Senegal	2007	Construction	Build the e-government network	Ex-Im Bank, China	Huawei; CMEC	—	51	51
Sierra Leone	2005	Completed	Provision of CDMA fixed-wireless network to government-owned Sierratel	Ex-Im Bank, China	Huawei	100	17	17

Country	Year	Status	Project	Chinese financier	Contractors	Added capacity	Project cost (US$ m)	Chinese commitments (US$ m)
Sierra Leone	2006	Construction	Upgrade the rural telecom network	Ex-Im Bank, China	Huawei	—	—	18
Sudan	2005	Agreement	Sudan Telecom purchasing equipment from ZTE	Ex-Im Bank, China	ZTE	—	—	200
Togo	2005	Completed	Expansion and upgrade the GSM network of Togo Cellulaire	Ex-Im Bank, China	ASB	100	17	Unconfirmed
Zambia	2006	Construction	Deploy fiber-optic lines over ZESCO power transmission network	Unknown	ZTE	—	11	—
Zimbabwe	2004	Construction	Two contracts for telecom equipment supply with Zimbabwe's state-owned, fixed-line operator TelOne and mobile operator NetOne	Ex-Im Bank, China	Huawei	—	332	Unconfirmed
ICT TOTAL								**2,774**

Source: World Bank–PPIAF Chinese Projects Database (2008).

a. Part of US$1.5 billion Ethiopia Millennium Project.

Table A3.4: Overview of Chinese financing commitments in confirmed water projects in sub-Saharan Africa, 2001–07

Country	Year	Status	Project	Chinese financier	Contractors	Added capacity	Project cost (US$ m)	Chinese commitments (US$ m)
Angola	2004	Completed	Water portion of the first phase of 2004 US$2 billion loan from Ex-Im Bank of China	Ex-Im Bank, China	Multiple	—	—	200
Cameroon	2007	Construction	Build a water treatment plant and water distribution pipeline in Douala	Ex-Im Bank, China	China Geo-Engineering Corporation (CGC)	—	—	24
Cape Verde	2004	Completed	Construction of the Poilco dam, largest dam project in the country	Government, China	Guangdong Yuanda Water Conservancy; Hydro Power Group Co., Ltd.	1,700,000 square meters	—	—
Congo, Rep. of	2005	Completed	Sibiti water supply project WIETC	Government, China		—	6	5.79
Congo, Rep. of	2005	Completed	Mosaka water supply project	Government, China	WIETC	—	2	1.65
Congo, Rep. of	2007	Construction	Rehabilitation of the old water treatment plant	Ex-Im Bank, China	CMEC	177,000 tons per day	—	—

Country	Year	Status	Project	Chinese financier	Contractors	Added capacity	Project cost (US$ m)	Chinese commitments (US$ m)
Mauritius	2007	Construction	Build a water treatment plant and the water distribution network	Ex-Im Bank, China	Beijing Construction Engineering Group	29,000 connections	—	63.75
Mozam-bique	2006	Agreement	Construction of the Moamba-Major dam in the Maputo province for drinking water supply	Ex-Im Bank, China	Unknown	—	300	—
Niger	2002	Completed	Niger Water Sector project to reinforce the water production system of Zinder	Government, China	China Railway Construction Corporation (CRCC)	600 cubic meters	9	4
Nigeria	2005	Completed	Construction of water schemes and water points for 19 states and the Federal Capital Territory	Government, China	Beijing G and M Construction Company Ltd.	—	5	—
Sudan	2005	Construction	Water supplying systems of Gedarif and Al-Fashir	Ex-Im Bank, China	China National Construction & Agricultural Machinery Imp./Exp. Corporation (CAMC)	—	100	—

(continued)

Table A3.4: *continued*

Country	Year	Status	Project	Chinese financier	Contractors	Added capacity	Project cost (US$ m)	Chinese commitments (US$ m)
Sudan	2006	Construction	Wad Medani Water Treatment Plant	Ex-Im Bank, China	CAMC	100,000 tons per day	29	—
Tanzania	2001	Completed	Chalinze (Shalinze) Water Supply Project, Phase 1	Government, China	Unknown	—	100	21
Tanzania	2003	Completed	Dodoma Water Supply Project	Government, China	China Civil Engineering Construction Company (CCECC)	—	77	—
Tanzania	2007	Construction	Grant to rehabilitate and extend the water supply system in Chalinze	Ministry of Commerce, China	Unknown	—	—	—
WATER TOTAL								**320**

Source: World Bank–PPIAF Chinese Projects Database (2008).

Table A3.5: Overview of Chinese financing commitments in confirmed multisector projects in sub-Saharan Africa, 2001–07

Country	Year	Status	Project	Chinese financier	Contractors	Added capacity (US$ m)	Project cost (US$ m)	Chinese commitments (US$ m)
Nigeria	2006	Construction	Lekki Free Trade Zone in Lagos, Phase 1 (power plants, road network, manufacturing facilities)	CCECC-Beyond International Investment & Development Co., Lekki Global Development Investment Co.	CCECC-Beyond International Investment & Development Co., Lekki Global Investment Co.	—	300	200
Angola	2004	Completed	Remaining public works portion of the first phase of 2004 US$2 billion loan from Ex-Im Bank of China	Ex-Im Bank, China	Unknown	—	—	30
Angola	2007	Agreement	Unallocated US$2 billion China Ex-Im Bank loan of 2007 (for infrastructure)	Ex-Im Bank, China	Unknown	—	—	2,000
MULTISECTOR TOTAL								**2,230**

Source: World Bank–PPIAF Chinese Projects Database (2008).

SUMMARY OF CHINESE-FUNDED INFRASTRUCTURE PROJECTS FOR SELECTED COUNTRIES

Table A4.1: Chinese financing commitments in infrastructure projects in Nigeria, 2001–07

Year	Status	Project	Sector	Chinese financier	Contractors	Added capacity	Project cost (US$ m)	Chinese commitments (US$ m)
2002	Construction	National Rural Telephony Project (NRPT), Phase 1	ICT	Ex-Im Bank, China	Huawei; ZTE; Alcatel Shanghai Bell (ASB)	150,226 conn.	200	200
2005	Construction	Construction of Papalanto power gas turbine plant in Ogun[a]	Electricity	Ex-Im Bank, China	Shandong Electric Power Constr. Corp. (SEPCO)	670 MW	360	298
2006	Construction	Lekki Free Trade Zone in Lagos, Phase 1; the funds will be used on power plants, road networks, and manufacturing facilities	Multiple	CCECC-Beyond International Investment & Development	CCECC-Beyond International Investment & Development	—	300	200
2006	Distressed	Modernization of the Nigeria railway, Phase 1: Lagos-Kano railway	Transport	Ex-Im Bank, China	China Civil Engineering Construction Company (CCECC)	1,315 km	8,300	2,500
2006	Completed	Nigeria First Communication Sattelite NigComSat-1	ICT	Ex-Im Bank, China	China Great Wall Industry Corporation	—	—	200

Year	Status	Project	Sector	Chinese financier	Contractors	Added capacity	Project cost (US$ m)	Chinese commitments (US$ m)
2006	Construction	Abuja Rail Mass Transit Project	Transport	Ex-Im Bank, China	China Guangdong Xinguang International Group	—	2,000	1,000
2006	Distressed	Construction of Mambilla hydroelectric power plant in Taraba state	Electricity	Ex-Im Bank, China	China Gezhouba Group Corporation (CGGC); China Geo-Engineering Corporation (CGC)	2,600 MW	1,460	1,000
NIGERIA TOTAL								**5,398**

Source: World Bank–PPIAF Chinese Projects Database (2008).

a. Chinese financing commitments for the other two plants Omotosho and Geregu are not confirmed (see table A3.1).

Table A4.2: Chinese financing commitments in infrastructure projects in Angola, 2001–07

Year	Status	Project	Sector	Chinese financier	Contractors	Added capacity	Project cost (US$ m)	Chinese commitments (US$ m)
2002	Completed	Rehabilitation and extension of the electrical system in Luanda, Phase 1	Electricity	Ex-Im Bank, China	China Machine-Building International Corporation (CMIC)	—	15	15
2003	Completed	Rehabilitation of Luanda railway, Phase 1	Transport	Government, China	China National Machinery & Equipment Import & Export Corporation (CMEC)	43 km	90	90
2004	Construction	The no. 1 and 2 ring roads of the Angola City[a]	Transport	Ex-Im Bank, China	CMEC	51.25 km	170	170
2004	Completed	Power portion of the first phase of 2004 US$2 billion loan from Ex-Im Bank of China[a]	Electricity	Ex-Im Bank, China	Multiple	—	—	200

(continued)

Table A4.2: *continued*

Year	Status	Project	Sector	Chinese financier	Contractors	Added capacity	Project cost (US$ m)	Chinese commitments (US$ m)
2004	Completed	Water portion of the first phase of 2004 US$2 billion loan from Ex-Im Bank of China[a]	Water	Ex-Im Bank, China	Multiple	—	—	200
2004	Completed	Remaining public works portion of the first phase of 2004 US$2 billion loan from Ex-Im Bank of China	Multiple	Ex-Im Bank, China	Multiple	—	—	301
2004	Completed	Telecom portion of the second phase of 2004 US$2 billion loan from Ex-Im Bank of China[a]	ICT	Ex-Im Bank, China	Multiple	—	—	200
2005	Construction	Rehabilitation of the Kifangondo-Caxito-Uige-Negage road[a]	Transport	Ex-Im Bank, China	China Road and Bridge Corporation (CRBC)	371 km	211	211
2005	Completed	An agreement between ZTE and Mundo Startel to install a new fixed-line network in 8 states across Angola	ICT	Ex-Im Bank, China	Zhong Xing Telecommunication Equipment Company Limited (ZTE)	—	69	38

Year	Status	Project	Sector	Chinese financier	Contractors	Added capacity	Project cost (US$ m)	Chinese commitments (US$ m)
2005	Completed	Rehabilitation and extension of the electrical system in Luanda, Phase 2	Electricity	Ex-Im Bank, China	CMIC	—	46	46
2007	Agreement	Unallocated US$2 billion China Ex-Im Bank Loan of 2007	Multiple	Ex-Im Bank, China	Multiple	—	—	2,000
ANGOLA TOTAL								**3,200**

Source: World Bank–PPIAF Chinese Projects Database (2008).

a. Part of 2004 China Ex-Im Bank credit line.

Table A4.3: Chinese financing commitments in infrastructure projects in Ethiopia, 2001–07

Year	Status	Project	Sector	Chinese financier	Contractors	Added capacity	Project cost (US$ m)	Chinese commitments (US$ m)
2002	Construction	Construction of the Tekeze Dam, in the state of Tigray in Ethiopia	Electricity	Ex-Im Bank, China	China National Water Resources and Hydropower Engineering Corporation (CWHEC)	300 MW	224	50
2003	Completed	Gottera-Wolo Sefer Road	Transport	Government, China	China Road and Bridge Corporation (CRBC)	2.6 km	4.52	2.94
2004	Completed	Addis Ababa city ring road, Phase 2	Transport	Government, China	CRBC	33.4 km	77	12.89
2006	Agreement	Road and two bridges construction in Addis Ababa	Transport	Government, China	CRBC	5.8 km	16.8	6.33
2006	Agreement	Expand and upgrade Ethiopia's telecom network[a]	ICT	Ex-Im Bank, China	Zhong Xing Tele-communication Equipment Company Limited (ZTE)	8,500,000 conn.[b]	—	822

Year	Status	Project	Sector	Chinese financier	Contractors	Added capacity	Project cost (US$ m)	Chinese commitments (US$ m)
2006	Construction	Construction of the Gotera intersection bridge in Addis Ababa	Transport	Ex-Im Bank, China	Shanghai Construction Group	—	12.71	12.71
2007	Construction	First phase of fiber trans-mission backbone, expansion of mobile phone service for the Ethiopian millennium and expansion of wireless telephone service[a]	ICT	Ex-Im Bank, China	ZTE	—	200	200
2007	Construction	GSM project phase II[a]	ICT	Ex-Im Bank, China	ZTE	—	478	478
ETHIOPIA TOTAL								**1,585**

Source: World Bank–PPIAF Chinese Projects Database (2008).

a. Part of US$ 1,5 billion Ethiopia Millennium Project

b. Refers to the total new connections under Ethiopia Millennium Project.

Table A4.4: Chinese financing commitments in infrastructure projects in Sudan, 2001–07

Year	Status	Project	Sector	Chinese financier	Contractors	Added capacity	Project cost (US$ m)	Chinese commitments (US$ m)
2001	Completed	Construction of the El-Gaili combined-cycle power Plant, Phase 1	Electricity	Ex-Im Bank, China	Harbin Power Equipment Company Limited	200 MW	150	128
2003	Construction	Construction of the Merowe hydroelectric dam (1,250 MW)[a]	Electricity	Ex-Im Bank, China	China Hydraulic and Hydroelectric Construction Group Corporation (Sinohydro Corporation)	1,250 MW	1,200	400
2004	Construction	Construction of the bridge between Khartoum and the Sudanese-Egyptian border	Transport	China National Petroleum Corporation (CNPC)	Jilin Province International Economy & Trade Development Corporation (JIETDC)	0.44 km	20	10
2005	Agreement	500 MW coal-fired power plant in Port Sudan; 320 MW gas-fired power plant in Rabak; 300 MW gas-fired Al Fula plant[b]	Electricity	Ex-Im Bank, China	Shandong Electric Power Construction Corporation	1,120 MW	—	512

Year	Status	Project	Sector	Chinese financier	Contractors	Added capacity	Project cost (US$ m)	Chinese commitments (US$ m)
2005	Agreement	Sudan Telecom purchasing equipment from ZTE	Telecom	Ex-Im Bank, China	ZTE	—	—	200
2006	Construction	National Electricity Corporation of Sudan (NEC)	Electricity	Ex-Im Bank, China	China National Machinery & Equipment Import & Export Corporation (CMEC)	340 km	81	81
SUDAN TOTAL								**1,330.5**

Source: World Bank–PPIAF Chinese Projects Database (2008).

a. The projects is cofinanced by Abu Dhabi Fund; Arab Bank for Economic Development in Africa (BADEA); Kuwait Fund for Arab Economic Development (KFAED); and the Saudi Fund for Development.

b. Construction of Al Fula plant commenced in 2007.

SUMMARY OF CHINESE-FUNDED NATURAL RESOURCE PROJECTS

Table A5.1: Chinese financing interests in confirmed natural resource projects

Country	Year	Project	Sector	Subsector	Financiers or sponsors	Project cost (US$ m)	Chinese commitments (US$ m)
Angola	2003	In 2003, Sinopec acquired block 3 in Angola	Oil	Exploration	China Petroleum and Chemical Corporation (SINOPEC)	—	—
Angola	2006	Sonaref: development of the refinery in Lobito by SSI, canceled	Oil	Refinery	Sonangol Sinopec International (SSI)	3,000	canceled
Angola	2006	Explore crude oil in Angola's three offshore oil fields (blocks 15, 17, 18)	Oil	Exploration	SINOPEC	2,400	2,400
Central African Republic	2007	Concession for oil block B in northeast near borders with Chad and Sudan	Oil	Exploration	China Poly Group Corporation; IAS International Holding Co.	—	—
Chad	2003	Purchase of a 50 percent stake in oil block H from Cliveden Petroleum of the United Kingdom by CITIC and CNPC	Oil	Exploration	China National Petroleum Corporation (CNPC); China International Trust and Investment Corporation (CITIC)	45	—

(continued)

Table A5.1: *continued*

Country	Year	Project	Sector	Subsector	Financiers or sponsors	Project cost (US$ m)	Chinese commitments (US$ m)
Chad	2006	Purchase of 50 percent stake in oil block from Canadian EnCana (Permit H)	Oil	Exploration	CNPC	203	203
Chad	2007	Build first oil refinery in Chad to the north of N'Djamena	Oil	Refinery	CNPC	—	
Congo, Dem. Rep. of	2003	New copper alloy and cobalt plant in Katanga	Minerals	Copper	Wambao Resources	—	—
Congo, Dem. Rep. of	2004	Rent 3 copper mines and collect cobalt	Minerals	Copper, cobalt	Xinglong Bicycle Co. Ltd.	—	—
Congo, Dem. Rep. of	2005	Development of Musonoi copper and cobalt mine	Minerals	Copper, cobalt	China National Overseas Engineering Corporation (COVEC)	—	100
Congo, Dem. Rep. of	2005	Establish a joint venture, Huaxin Mines Co. Ltd.	Minerals	Copper	Shanghai Industrial Investment (Holdings) Co. Ltd.	—	—
Congo, Dem. Rep. of	2006	Develop the Kalumbwe-Myunga copper-cobalt mine	Minerals	Copper, cobalt	China Railway Engineering Group Co. Ltd. (CREGC); Ex-Im Bank, China	270	270

Country	Year	Project	Sector	Subsector	Financiers or sponsors	Project cost (US$ m)	Chinese commitments (US$ m)
Congo, Dem. Rep. of	2007	Purchase of the prospecting and mining rights to a cobalt mine in Lubumbashi	Minerals	Cobalt	Dalian Xinyang High-Tech Development (DLX)	2	Unconfirmed
Congo, Rep. of	2005	Two oil field concessions: Marine XII and Haute Mer B.	Oil	Exploration	SINOPEC	—	—
Côte d'Ivoire	2005	Manganese ore project	Minerals	Manganese	China National Geological and Mining Corporation	—	—
Equatorial Guinea	2006	Exploration of oil block S	Oil	Exploration	China National Offshore Oil Corporation (CNOOC)	—	—
Eritrea	2006	Exploration rights for copper mine	Minerals	Copper	China National Geological and Mining Corporation	—	—
Eritrea	2006	Jointly develop a gold mine	Minerals	Gold	China National Geological and Mining Corporation	—	—
Eritrea	2007	Explore gold and copper in Kenatib and Defere	Minerals	Copper, gold	Beijing Southeast Resources Company Limited	—	—

(continued)

Table A5.1: *continued*

Country	Year	Project	Sector	Subsector	Financiers or sponsors	Project cost (US$ m)	Chinese commitments (US$ m)
Eritrea	2007	China Ex-Im Bank provided a commercial loan of US$60 million to the Eritrea government, which spent the loan to acquire 40 percent of the Bisha project from a Canadian company Nevsun	Minerals	Copper, gold	Ex-Im Bank, China	60	60
Eritrea	2007	Explore and develop minerals in Augaro (Gash-Barka Region)	Minerals	Multiple	China National Geological and Mining Corporation	—	—
Gabon	2004	Technical evaluation of three onshore oil fields (one oil and two gas blocks)	Oil	Exploration	SINOPEC	—	—
Gabon	2005	SINOPEC purchased Block G4–188 from Transworld	Oil	Exploration	SINOPEC	—	—
Gabon	2005	Exploration of Mbigou manganese mine	Minerals	Manganese	Sino Steel	—	—

Country	Year	Project	Sector	Subsector	Financiers or sponsors	Project cost (US$ m)	Chinese commitments (US$ m)
Gabon	2005	Exploration work on a manganese ore deposit in the vicinity of Mont Bembele, near the north-western town of Ndjolé (Moyen-Ogooué Province)	Minerals	Manganese	Xuzhou Huayan; Ningbo Huaneng Kuangye	—	2
Gabon	2006	Exploration of block G4–217 (1815.3 km²)	Oil	Exploration	SINOPEC	—	—
Gabon	2006	License for Njielei Manganese mines	Minerals	Manganese	Ningbo Huazhou mines	—	—
Gabon	2006	Exploration license for 2000 km² of deposit with lead, zinc, and silver	Minerals	Lead, zinc, silver	Ningbo Huazhou mines	—	—
Gabon	2006	Belinga iron ore project; includes construction of Poubara hydropower dam, Belinga-Santa Clara railway, and deep-water port at Santa Clara	Minerals	Iron	Financing by China Ex-Im Bank; Mining by Panzhihua Iron & Steel Co.	3,000	—

(continued)

Table A5.1: *continued*

Country	Year	Project	Sector	Subsector	Financiers or sponsors	Project cost (US$ m)	Chinese commitments (US$ m)
Guinea	2005	Renewable 3-year bauxite exploration license	Minerals	Bauxite	Aluminium Corp of China	—	63
Guinea	2007	Exploration of aluminum in Boke district, Guinea	Minerals	Aluminium	China Henan International Cooperation Group (CHICO); Henan Provincial State-Owned Assets Operation Company; Henan Zhonglian Mining Co., Ltd.; Yongcheng Coal & Electricity Holding Group Co., Ltd.	—	—
Kenya	2006	Production-sharing contracts for six onshore blocks (1, 9, 10A, L2, L3, and L4)	Oil	Exploration	China National Offshore Oil Corporation (CNOOC)	—	—
Kenya	2006	Purchase the debenture of Tiomin Kenya	Minerals	Titanium	Jinchuan Group Limited (JNMC)	—	—
Kenya	2007	Financing titanium project in Kwale district with Tiomin	Minerals	Titanium	JNMC	155	24
Liberia	2006	Explore petroleum in Liberia	Oil	Exploration	SINOPEC	—	—

Country	Year	Project	Sector	Subsector	Financiers or sponsors	Project cost (US$ m)	Chinese commitments (US$ m)
Madagascar	2007	Exploration of oil block 3,113	Oil	Exploration	Sino Union Petroleum & Chemical International	103	103
Mali	2004	Exploration license for four to five blocks in the areas of Timbuktu and Gao	Oil	Exploration	SINOPEC	—	—
Mauritania	2004	Exploration of block 12 and two areas in block 13	Oil	Exploration	China National Petroleum Corporation (CNPC)	—	—
Mauritania	2005	65 percent stake in oil and gas exploration in block 20	Oil	Exploration	CNPC	—	9
Mozambique	2003	Exploration licenses for Manica	Minerals	Gold	Jiangsu Geology & Mineral Resources Bureau	—	—
Mozambique	2004	Subcontract to build 9 oil product storage tanks	Oil	Other	CNPC	220	—
Multiple countries	2006	The state-owned bank funded a purchase of 1.1 percent of Anglo by China Vision Resources Ltd, the investment vehicle of Chinese billionaire Larry Yung	Minerals	Multiple	China Vision Resources with financing from China Development Bank (CDB)	—	783

(continued)

Table A5.1: *continued*

Country	Year	Project	Sector	Subsector	Financiers or sponsors	Project cost (US$ m)	Chinese commitments (US$ m)
Namibia	2005	Permits for four prospecting licenses for deposits of copper, lead, zinc, silver, gold, uranium, and stone	Minerals	Copper, lead, zinc, silver, gold, uranium, stone	Namibia (China) Mining Resources Investment and Development Co. Ltd.	—	—
Niger	2003	License for the exploration of block BILMA	Oil	Exploration	CNPC	—	—
Niger	2006	Drill exploration wells in Tenere oil block	Oil	Exploration	CNPC	44	Unconfirmed
Niger	2006	Explore Teguidda and Madaouela uranium mineral deposits	Minerals	Uranium	China Nuclear International Uranium Corporation (Sino U); ZXJOY Invest	—	—
Niger	2007	Develop Azelik uranium mineral deposit in Agadez region	Minerals	Uranium	Sino U	335	—
Nigeria	2004	Oil exploration contract for blocks 64 and 66 in the Chad Basin	Oil	Exploration	SINOPEC	2,270	Unconfirmed

Building Bridges: China's Growing Role as Infrastructure Financier for Sub-Saharan Africa

Country	Year	Project	Sector	Subsector	Financiers or sponsors	Project cost (US$ m)	Chinese commitments (US$ m)
Nigeria	2006	45 percent of interest in an offshore oil exploitation license OML130, which comprises Akpo Oilfield and 3 other discoveries	Oil	Exploration	CNOOC	2268	2,692
Nigeria	2006	35 percent working interest in the Nigeria OPL 229	Oil	Exploration	CNOOC	—	60
Nigeria	2006	Acquisition of a 51 percent stake in the Kaduna refinery and rehabilitation	Oil	Refinery	CNPC	—	2,000
Nigeria	2006	License for 4 oil blocks OPL 471, 721, 732, and 298	Oil	Exploration	CNPC	16	Unconfirmed
Nigeria	2006	Provide seismic exploration service	Oil	Exploration	SINOPEC	—	10
Nigeria	2006	Negotiating with Nigeria on the priority rights to purchase offshore blocks	Oil	Exploration	CNOOC	—	—
Nigeria	2006	Asphalite mine	Minerals	Asphalite	SINOPEC	—	19

(continued)

Table A5.1: *continued*

Country	Year	Project	Sector	Subsector	Financiers or sponsors	Project cost (US$ m)	Chinese commitments (US$ m)
Nigeria	2007	CNOOC was granted four oil districts	Oil	Exploration	CNOOC	—	—
Nigeria	2007	Three development projects for sugar, hydropower, and solid minerals in Zamfara state	Multiple	Hydro-power, minerals, and sugar	Reofield Industries Ltd	300	—
Nigeria	2007	Exploration of solid minerals in Zamfara and oil in the northwestern Nigerian Sokoto Basin	Multiple	Oil and solid minerals	Zhognho Overseas Construction Engineering Company Limited	300	300
São Tomé and Príncipe	2006	License for block 2 in the Gulf of Guinea Joint Development Zone (JDZ)	Oil	Exploration	SINOPEC	17.75	Unconfirmed
South Africa	2006	Chromium development project, which includes one mine and a concentration factory	Minerals	Chromium	Jiuquan Iron & Steel company (JISCO)	—	330

Country	Year	Project	Sector	Subsector	Financiers or sponsors	Project cost (US$ m)	Chinese commitments (US$ m)
South Africa	2006	Purchase 50 percent share in chromium and smelteries from Samancor Chrome	Minerals	Chromium	Sino Steel	—	200
South Africa	2007	Exploration of chromium in Naboom in South Africa	Minerals	Chromium	Minmetals Development Co., Ltd.	—	7
South Africa	2007	South African ferro-chrome project, Phase 2	Minerals	Iron, chromium	JISCO	510	510
Sudan	2001	Heglig and Unity oil fields (blocks 1, 2, and 4)	Oil	Exploration	CNPC	144	Unconfirmed
Sudan	2002	Petrodar Operating Company, developing blocks 3 and 7	Oil	Exploration	CNPC	—	—
Sudan	2003	Expand the capacity of Khartoum refinery	Oil	Refinery	CNPC	150	Unconfirmed
Sudan	2003	Exploration of the Tiki-1 Test Well in 3/7 Oil Area	Oil	Exploration	Zhongyuan Petroleum Exploration Bureau (ZPEB)	1	Unconfirmed

(continued)

Table A5.1: continued

Country	Year	Project	Sector	Subsector	Financiers or sponsors	Project cost (US$ m)	Chinese commitments (US$ m)
Sudan	2003	Construction of a 750 km 200,000 b/d pipeline to move oil from block 6 in the southern Kordofan field to the Khartoum refinery and north to Port Sudan	Oil	Distribution	CNPC	350	Unconfirmed
Sudan	2005	Exploration of offshore gas block 15 within the Red Sea Basin	Natural gas	Exploration	CNPC	20	—
Sudan	2006	Explore gold in a 6,000 km² field	Minerals	Gold	North China Geological Exploration Bureau	—	4
Sudan	2007	40 percent stake in block 13, off the coast of the Red Sea	Oil	Exploration	CNPC	—	—
Tanzania	2006	Technical support service to expand the production capacity of a coal mine	Minerals	Coal	Shanxi Fenwei Energy Consulting Co., Ltd.	—	—

Country	Year	Project	Sector	Subsector	Financiers or sponsors	Project cost (US$ m)	Chinese commitments (US$ m)
Zambia	2003	Coal mine at the old Nkandabbwe mine in Sinazongwe district	Minerals	Coal	Collum Coal Mining Industries Limited	25	Unconfirmed
Zambia	2004	Develop manganese mine near industrial town Kabwe	Minerals	Manganese	Chiman Manufacturing Ltd.	10	Unconfirmed
Zambia	2005	Construction of wet-process smelting plant and sulfur-to-acid plant at Chambishi copper mine	Minerals	Copper smelter plant	China Nonferrous Metal Mining (Group) Co. Ltd. (CNMC)	20	20
Zambia	2006	Construction of the Chambishi Copper Smelter	Minerals	Copper smelter plant	CNMC; Yunnan Copper Industry (Group) Co. Ltd. (YNCIG)	200	100
Zambia	2006	Munali Nickel Project	Minerals	Nickel	Jinchuan Group Limited (JNMC)	—	25
Zambia	2007	Chambishi West Ore Body Project	Minerals	Copper	CNMC	100	100

(continued)

Table A5.1: *continued*

Country	Year	Project	Sector	Subsector	Financiers or sponsors	Project cost (US$ m)	Chinese commitments (US$ m)
Zimbabwe	2007	Acquisition of 92 percent in Mauritius-based company ZCE, the owner of the Zimbabwe's largest chromium producer Zimasco, by Sino Steel	Minerals	Chromium	Sino Steel; Sino-Africa Fund	—	200
Zimbabwe	2007	Develop coal in Zimbabwe	Minerals	Coal	Sanxing Coal	—	—
Zimbabwe	2007	A joint venture with Zimbabwe National Power Company to develop and operate the Sinamatella Coal Field and coal fields in western Zimbabwe	Minerals	Coal	China National Aero-Technology Import & Export Co. (CATIC); Pingdingshan Coal (Group) Co., Ltd.	—	—
NATURAL RESOURCES TOTAL							**10,591**

Source: World Bank–PPIAF Chinese Projects Database (2008).

INDEX

mineral development, 44

natural resource commitments increase, 43

natural resource imports, 39f, 42f

natural resource projects, 121t–134t

natural resource requirements, xv–xvi

oil exploration, 50

oil imports by source, 40f

oil sector investment in Africa, 39–40, 44, 49b–50b

project values, 33–34

projects verified, 15f

telecom firms, 24

trade, 3, 4, 4f, 39, 41t

China Africa Development Fund, 53f

China Development Bank (CDB), 52

China Machine-Building International Corporation (CMIC), 22

China National Machinery & Equipment Import & Export Corp. (CMEC), 22

China National Offshore Oil Corporation (CNOOC), 43, 49b

China National Petroleum Corporation (CNPC , also PetroChina), 26, 49b

China Road and Bridge Corporation (CRBC), 24

China-Africa Business Council (CABC), 6b

China-Congo Telecom (CCT) network project, 101t

Chinese Journal Web, 12

Chinese Transtech Engineering Corporation, 23

chromium ore, 41t

civil works contracts captured by foreign contractors, 35f

coal, 44

cobalt ore, 41t

Collum Mine, 44

Comoros, 93t

complementarities of Africa and China, 29–30, 29t, 74

complementarities, Africa and China, xiv–xv

concessional loans, 53–55, 60

Congo River Dam, 21, 86t

Congo, Democratic Republic of, 36f, 101t

natural resource commitments, 47f

projects, 122t–123t

Congo, Republic of, 37, 40f, 86t

airport projects, 93t

resource-backed infrastructure projects, 57t

road projects, 97t

water project financing commitments, 106t

contractors, 19, 20t, 36, 83–84, xv

copper ore, 41t

Côte d'Ivoire, 101t, 123t

country indebtedness, 62–64

CRBC. *See* China Road and Bridge Corporation

Dande, Zimbabwe, 90t

data collection, 12, 79–81

data sources, 9–11

debt relief, 62–64, 65t, xviii

Debtor Reporting System (DRS), 12, 58

development assistance, Chinese approach to, 1–2, 8, 73, xiii, xvi

Dodoma Water Supply Project, 108t

East Asia and Pacific (EAP), 30t, 32t, 40f

ECA. *See* Export Credit Agreement

economic complementarities, 29–30, 29t, xiv–xv

economic cooperation, 9–10, 10f

economic growth, hindered by inadequate infrastructure, 31–32

Harbin Power Equipment Company, 22, 28
Huawei, 24, 25
Hwange Power Station, 90t
hydrocarbon resources, 43
hydropower projects, 21, 28, 86t–88t, xiii

India, 67, 68, 69f, 73, xviii
information and communications technology (ICT) sector, 22f, 25, 31, 36f, Xiii
   development indicators, 30t
   Ethiopia, 24, 27
   financing, 70, 70f
   grant-financed projects, 59t
   projects, 100t–105t
   sources of financing, 71f
information collection with Factiva database, 79–81
information sources, 9–11
infrastructure deficit, 74
infrastructure development indicators, 30–33, 30t
infrastructure financing, 11t, 16, 73. *See also* China; loans
   and corresponding natural resource investments, 47
   between lower-income countries, 7–8
   by country, 26f
   by sector, 70
   by source and type, 53f
   complementarity of focus by sources, xviii–xix
   external by sector, 70f
   gaps, 33
   internal, 69f
   multisector projects, 109t
   non-OECD, 66, 69f, 71, 72f

   OECD compared to non-OECD, 68, 70–72
   sectoral specialization, 71f
infrastructure inadequacy, 31–32, 47
infrastructure investment needs, 33, 34t, xv
infrastructure investment pays off, 31
infrastructure projects, 2, 13, 22, 34, xii, xviii–xix
   Angola, 113t–115t
   by year and status, 19f
   contracted out to Chinese construction firms, 34, 55–56
   country-by-country, 25–28
   data verification, 14
   database construction, xii
   Ethiopia, 116t–117t
   geographic distribution of, xiv
   grant-financed, 58, 59t
   linked to resource development, 48t
   multisectoral, 109t
   natural resource and political considerations, 84
   new and size distribution, 18f
   Nigeria, 111t–112t
   resource-backed, 57t
   rise in and classification of, 17–19
   sectoral distribution of, 19, 20t, 21–25, xiii–xiv
   Sudan, 118t–119t
   value of projects financed by China, 10
infrastructure projects database, 11–15, 15f
   constructed with the Factiva database, 79–81
   information included in, 82–84
infrastructure services costlier, 31
infrastructure services' reliability, 32–33, 32t